BECOMING ACTIVE CITIZENS

*Practices to Engage Students in
Civic Education Across the Curriculum*

TOM DRISCOLL SHAWN W. McCUSKER

Solution Tree | Press

Copyright © 2022 by Solution Tree Press

All rights reserved, including the right of reproduction of this book in whole or in part in any form.

555 North Morton Street
Bloomington, IN 47404
800.733.6786 (toll free) / 812.336.7700
FAX: 812.336.7790

email: info@SolutionTree.com
SolutionTree.com

Printed in the United States of America

Library of Congress Cataloging-in-Publication Data

Names: Driscoll, Tom, 1985- author. | McCusker, Shawn W., author.
Title: Becoming active citizens : practices to engage students in civic
   education across the curriculum / Tom Driscoll, Shawn W. McCusker.
Description: Bloomington, IN : Solution Tree Press, [2022] | Includes
   bibliographical references and index.
Identifiers: LCCN 2021056600 (print) | LCCN 2021056601 (ebook) | ISBN
   9781952812934 (paperback) | ISBN 9781952812941 (ebook)
Subjects: LCSH: Civics--Study and teaching. | Citizenship--Study and
   teaching. | Political sociology.
Classification: LCC LC1091 .D73 2022 (print) | LCC LC1091 (ebook) | DDC
   370.11/5--dc23/eng/20220511
LC record available at https://lccn.loc.gov/2021056600
LC ebook record available at https://lccn.loc.gov/2021056601

Solution Tree
Jeffrey C. Jones, CEO
Edmund M. Ackerman, President

Solution Tree Press
President and Publisher: Douglas M. Rife
Associate Publisher: Sarah Payne-Mills
Managing Production Editor: Kendra Slayton
Editorial Director: Todd Brakke
Art Director: Rian Anderson
Copy Chief: Jessi Finn
Senior Production Editor: Christine Hood
Content Development Specialist: Amy Rubenstein
Proofreader: Elisabeth Abrams
Text and Cover Designer: Rian Anderson
Associate Editor: Sarah Ludwig
Editorial Assistants: Charlotte Jones and Elijah Oates

For my wife Michaela and children Blake and Lydia—you mean the world to me. For my parents, Tom and Lisa Driscoll, lifelong educators who inspired my devotion to the profession and encouraged my passion for writing. And for the teachers and civic leaders educating our next generation of citizens—your work has a powerful impact, and we appreciate all you do.

—Tom Driscoll

For Kristen, whose tireless love and support encourage me to say "yes" to new adventures. For Brian and Emily, who inspire me to imagine how things might be and work to create a better future. And to all the educators out there navigating the challenges of discussing civic education. It's worth it. Keep at it.

—Shawn W. McCusker

ACKNOWLEDGMENTS

We would first like to thank Sarah Jubar and Christine Hood of Solution Tree, who skillfully and enthusiastically guided us through this book project.

Thanks to the inspiring educators Marc LeBlanc and Jeff Grifka, who spent time meeting with us discussing their experiences with civic education. Thanks to Mike Trofi, a veteran educator and trainer for the Center for Civic Education, for sharing valuable perspectives on the historical trajectory of civic education and what works regarding professional development.

Thanks to education leaders Tom Vander Ark and Scott McLeod for providing valuable insights and pointing us in the direction of innovative schools and teachers across the United States.

Thanks to Mary Ellen Daneels for sharing her passion for civic education and her efforts to promote meaningful civic education in Illinois and beyond.

Thanks to the team at Kidizenship for meeting with us and sharing the vision and goals of your inspiring project that fosters civic engagement and creative self-expression.

Also, a big thanks to Anahita Dalmia and the team at Agents of Influence for meeting on several occasions to share ideas and discuss ways that their project can help enhance skills and competencies at the heart of civic education.

Thanks to Gail Ross-McBride and Tom Daccord for your encouragement and support to pursue our passions around civic education.

Solution Tree Press would like to thank the following reviewers:

David Bosso
Social Studies Teacher
Berlin High School
Berlin, Connecticut

Johanna Josaphat
Social Studies Teacher
The Urban Assembly Unison School
Brooklyn, New York

Shanna Martin
Social Studies and Technology Teacher,
    Instructional Coach
Lomira Middle School
Lomira, Wisconsin

Phil Strunk
History Teacher
Clarke County Public Schools
Berryville, Virginia

Sarah Carson Svendsen
Kindergarten Teacher,
    Instructional Coach
Pine Crest School
Boca Raton, Florida

Rosemarie Swallow
Social Studies and Reading Teacher
Lava Ridge Intermediate
Santa Clara, Utah

Neil Wrona
Social Studies Teacher and
    Technology Facilitator
Youth in Transition School
Baltimore, Maryland

TABLE OF CONTENTS

ABOUT THE AUTHORS xiii

INTRODUCTION 1
    The Need for Civic Education Reform 3
    About This Book 4

PART 1: THE STATE OF CIVIC EDUCATION 7

Chapter 1
HOW SCHOOLS PROVIDE CIVIC EDUCATION 9
    Modern Civic Engagement 10
    The Making of Good Citizens 11
    Traditional Civics Instruction 13
    Civic Education Requirements 15
    Conclusion 19
    Key Takeaways for How Schools Provide Civic Education 19

Chapter 2
WHAT WORKS IN CIVIC EDUCATION 21
    The Promise and Potential of Schools 22
    Implementation Strategies for Best Practices in Civic Education 25
        Courses on Civics, Government, Law, and Related Topics 25
        Deliberations of Current, Controversial Issues 26
        Service Learning 26

    Student Voice in Schools 27
    Simulations of Adult Civic Roles. 27
    High-Quality News Media Literacy Education 27
    Specific Focus on Action Civics. 28
    Increased Focus on Social-Emotional Learning 28
    School Climate Reform 29
Conclusion. 29
Key Takeaways for What Works in Civic Education 30

PART 2: MODERN CIVICS IN ACTION 31

Chapter 3
THE POWER OF ACTION CIVICS AND AUTHENTIC EXPERIENCES 33

The *Why* of Action Civics. 34
Action Civics and Deeper Learning 35
Action Civics Programs 36
    Generation Citizen 37
    Mikva Challenge. 37
    Project Citizen. 38
    Earth Force 38
Core Components of Quality Action Civics 38
Technologies to Enhance Action Civics. 40
    Online Research 40
    Collaboration, Deliberation, and Community Outreach 40
    Communication Tools for Advocacy 41
Action Civics in Action 42
    Generation Citizen Projects. 42
    Constitutional Rights Foundation Civic Action Projects. 44
    Mikva Challenge Action Civics Projects 44
Challenges of Action Civics. 45
Conclusion. 45
Key Takeaways for the Power of Action Civics and Authentic Experiences 46

Chapter 4
ENGAGEMENT IN CIVIL DISCOURSE 47

Why Many Teachers Don't Engage in Civil Discourse With Students 49
How to Teach Democratic Values Through Civil Discourse. 50
    Participate in Local Government 50
    Address Relevant, Real-Life Problems 51
    Debate Different Topics. 52
    Create Class Norms 53
    Participate in Class Dialogues. 54
    Engage in Virtual Discourse 55

         Complete Civic Action Projects. 57
         Explore Controversial Topics. 58
   Conclusion. 60
   Key Takeaways for Engagement in Civil Discourse 60

Chapter 5
NEWS MEDIA LITERACY FOR COMBATING MISINFORMATION 63
   The Dangers of Misinformation 65
   News Media Literacy Education. 66
   News Media Literacy Activities. 67
         Using Lateral Reading 68
         Understanding Bias 68
         Exposing the Motives of Misinformation 69
         Analyzing Historical Sources 70
         Navigating Digital Information 71
         Understanding the Power of Images. 71
   Tools to Enhance Online Research and Reasoning 72
         Pew Research Quiz. 72
         AllSides. 73
         Fact-Checking Tools. 73
   Conclusion. 74
   Key Takeaways for News Media Literacy for Combating Misinformation 75

Chapter 6
ENGAGEMENT THROUGH DIGITAL GAMES AND COMPETITIONS. 77
   Digital Games. 78
         iCivics. 78
         Games for Change 78
         Factitious 79
         Informable 79
         Lives in the Balance (iThrive Games). 80
   Competitions. 81
         We the People: Mock Congressional Hearing Competition 81
         Generation Citizen Civics Day Competition. 82
         Project Soapbox. 82
         Kidizenship Competitions. 83
         Games for Change (G4C) Student Competition 83
   Conclusion. 83
   Key Takeaways for Engagement Through Digital Games and Competitions. 84

PART 3: CIVICS LESSONS ACROSS SUBJECT AREAS 85

Chapter 7
CIVICS LESSONS FOR SOCIAL STUDIES 87
- Elementary Social Studies Lesson 88
  - Leaders in Our Community 88
- Secondary Social Studies Lesson 91
  - Gerrymandering in the United States: Curse or Blessing? 91
- Conclusion 95
- Key Takeaways for Civics Lessons for Social Studies 95

Chapter 8
CIVICS LESSONS FOR ENGLISH LANGUAGE ARTS 97
- Elementary English Language Arts Lesson 98
  - Opinion Writing and Revising for the Effective Use of Supporting Facts 98
- Secondary English Language Arts Lesson 103
  - The Power of Persuasion: Advocating for Change in the World 103
- Conclusion 106
- Key Takeaways for Civics Lessons for English Language Arts 106

Chapter 9
CIVICS LESSONS FOR SCIENCE AND MATHEMATICS 107
- Civics in Science 108
- Elementary Science Lesson 108
  - Community Solutions to Weather-Related Problems 108
- Secondary Science Lesson 112
  - Mitigating Human Impacts on Earth's Systems 112
- Civics in Mathematics 114
- Elementary Mathematics Lesson 115
  - Election Demographics 115
- Secondary Mathematics Lesson 118
  - Zip Code and Life Expectancy 118
- Conclusion 121
- Key Takeaways for Civics Lessons for Science and Mathematics 121

Chapter 10
INTERDISCIPLINARY CIVICS EXPERIENCES 123
- Elementary Interdisciplinary Civics Experience 123
  - Climate Science and Our School 124
- Secondary Interdisciplinary Civics Experience 129
  - The Policy, Politics, and Science of Vaccines 129
- Conclusion 135
- Key Takeaways for Interdisciplinary Civics Experiences 135

EPILOGUE 137
    A Call to Action for Teachers 139
    A Call to Action for School and District Leaders 140
    A Call to Action for Policymakers 140
    A Call to Action for Parents 141
    Conclusion 141

REFERENCES AND RESOURCES 143

INDEX 157

ABOUT THE AUTHORS

Tom Driscoll is an author, speaker, and educational consultant for EdTechTeacher, working with over two hundred client schools in the United States and internationally. He is a former digital learning director for the Bristol Warren Regional School District in Rhode Island, where he led numerous projects and initiatives related to the district's digital learning transformation. Tom began his career as a high school social studies teacher in two public school districts in Connecticut. Leveraging his extensive experience leading professional development around educational technology, personalization, design thinking, project-based learning, and civic education, Tom partners with schools and organizations around the world to design and implement innovative, student-centered learning environments.

Tom has presented at over fifty regional and national conferences and has authored several publications, including chapters for instructional technology titles published by ISTE and IGI Global, and contributed articles to media outlets such as Edutopia, EdSurge, EdTech K12, and *The New York Times*.

Tom was the recipient of the Rhode Island Department of Education's Digital Learning Champion for Leadership Award in 2016. He also is a Google for Education Certified Trainer, Newsela Certified Trainer, and Microsoft Innovative Educator.

Tom received a bachelor's degree in history from Vassar College and a master's degree in computing in education from Teachers College, Columbia University.

To learn more about Tom's work, visit www.TomDriscollEDU.com, or follow him @TomDriscollEDU on Twitter and Instagram.

Shawn W. McCusker is director of professional learning at Digital Promise, a nonprofit dedicated to closing the digital learning gap and supporting teachers in schools across the United States. Shawn has twenty-five years of experience as a teacher and leader in public, private, and alternative schools. He is passionate in his belief in student-centered, experiential learning and the power of student storytelling. He was an early innovator in the creation and organization of online learning communities via Twitter, such as #sschat and #1to1techat.

Shawn works with schools across the United States developing teacher capacity in technology use, blended learning, creativity, and engaging civic education strategies. He regularly presents on these topics at conferences across the United States.

As an expert in technology integration, his lessons and student products have been featured in *The Journal*, *Educational Leadership*, and *Education Week*. In 2006, he was recognized as a finalist for the Golden Apple Award for Excellence in Teaching. In 2016, he was named a Top Trailblazing Educator on Twitter by eSchoolNews.

Shawn received a bachelor of arts in history from Northern Illinois University and a master of arts in educational leadership from Concordia University Chicago.

To learn more about Shawn's work, visit https://gowhereyougrow.wordpress.com, or follow him @ShawnMcCusker on Twitter.

To book Tom Driscoll or Shawn W. McCusker for professional development, contact pd@SolutionTree.com.

INTRODUCTION

What is civic education?

According to the Annenberg Classroom (n.d.), *civic education* is "teaching the knowledge, skills, and virtues needed for competent citizenship in a democracy." One way of interpreting this definition is that civic education is providing each student with what they need to live in a democracy. Another is that we are preparing students to understand democracy so they can ensure it survives for future generations. Democracy and the skills to nurture it are not as easy to come by as you might think. Democracy is hard work. It demands a lot from its citizens in order to function properly.

It is for exactly this reason that Canadian psychologist Shawn Rosenberg (2019) predicts in his paper, "Democracy Devouring Itself: The Rise of the Incompetent Citizen and the Appeal of Populism," that democracy won't survive. His core argument is that democracy asks citizens to respect people with different backgrounds and beliefs. It requires them to sift through large amounts of information to determine what is right and what is wrong, and what is true and what is false. Democracy requires that citizens be thoughtful, disciplined, and logical (Shenkman, 2019). In Rosenberg's (2019) opinion, American democracy has a basic structural flaw. It has not successfully created the citizens it needs to survive. If it is to survive, it needs to immediately create citizens who have the cognitive and emotional capacities that democracy requires.

While we do not agree with Rosenberg that it's too late for democracy in the United States and the world, we do agree that we are not doing enough to prepare citizens. We need to fundamentally change how we approach the task. Most government instruction takes place in the form of lecture or discussion, without any interactive participation. In the United States, 70 percent of students will never write a letter, share an opinion, or help solve a problem as part of their civic education. Fifty-six percent of students will never take part in a mock trial or government simulation; fifty-three percent will never take a field trip or venture out of their classrooms; and thirty-one percent will complete their civic education without ever taking part in a debate (Hansen, Levesque, Valant, & Quintero, 2018). It seems that something key is missing from modern civic education—the part in which students get to actually *be citizens*.

If you wanted to teach someone to swim, how would you do it? How would you have him or her begin? The obvious answer—get him or her in a pool—seems pretty simple, right? Each year, millions of people learn to swim by getting in a pool, holding the side, and kicking furiously. Each year, parents and swim instructors get in a pool, hold out their arms, and beckon a soon-to-be swimmer to jump in. Eventually, these swimmers will have the confidence to take that leap for themselves.

Every day in the United States, on average, eleven people die from drowning, and twenty-two more people drown but are saved from death by a rescuer (Centers for Disease Control and Prevention, 2021). The main reason for these drownings, both fatal and nonfatal, is the lack of swimming ability. A contributing factor is the lack of access to pools and swimming instruction and the fear of deep water that results (Denny et al., 2019). African American children are more than five times more likely to drown than White children in the same age group due to a lack of basic skills that are the direct result of limited access to pools and swimming instruction in their communities (Gilchrist & Parker, 2014).

Similarly, the overall voting rates of Americans ages eighteen to twenty-four have been falling since 1964. The erosion and devaluation of civic education programs in schools are a contributing factor (Duer, 2016). Whether in pools or in politics, limited participation results in limited experience. Students with experience behave differently compared to those without it. To continue with the analogy, those with access to pools are more likely to swim. Those who receive high-quality civic education are more likely to vote, discuss politics, contact the government, and take part in other civic activities like volunteering (Guilfoile & Delander, 2014).

The trick is *being able to get in the water*. But let's say we, as educators, didn't have access to water. How would we teach students to swim and never once get in a pool? We could create lessons. We might have to rely on lectures. We could create a PowerPoint lesson on proper breathing and effective kicking. We could show them videos of Olympic athletes swimming and analyze their form. Advanced students who do well on the tests might take an advanced course on diving, and we could create a completely land-based course on lifeguarding.

Ridiculous, right? Would you want a student who had been through this type of training to jump into a pool? No, of course not.

And yet, this is exactly the model that we now use in schools to teach government and civics classes that are supposed to prepare students to become active, participating citizens in the world's greatest democracy. As you will see in chapter 1, the majority of civics instruction takes place in the classroom in the form of lecture or discussion. In most cases, schools are not required to have students participate in the processes of government or in any meaningful way. Much like in the swimming example, students merely hear about citizenship before they are asked to jump in and participate in democracy. It's as ridiculous as jumping in the pool after virtual swim lessons.

It doesn't have to be this way. We can do better. We know what better looks like. In simple terms, we need to "get students in the pool" and teach them what to do by having them *do* it.

The Need for Civic Education Reform

As of 2018, nine states in the United States did not have a civic education course requirement, including Alaska, Kentucky, Massachusetts, Montana, New Jersey, Oregon, Rhode Island, Vermont, and Washington (Hansen et al., 2018). Consider the level of confusion and frustration this could cause students who are not required to receive instruction on the structure, principles, and mechanisms of democracy and how it would prevent them from being able to engage in the processes of democracy in even the smallest way. Citizens won't value and respect democracy if they don't understand how the structure of the U.S. system was established to divide power and keep the reins of government in the hands of citizens rather than the hands of those who rise to power.

In 2003, the Carnegie Corporation of New York and Center for Information and Research on Civic Learning and Engagement (CIRCLE) published *The Civic Mission of Schools*, which lays out a vision of a richer, more meaningful approach to civic education in the United States. It identifies a growing trend of cynicism toward government institutions and civic engagement among U.S. students and, in general, U.S. society. The report states that schools have the powerful potential to address this trend by providing high-quality civic education programs and addressing the inequalities of civic and political education, and identifies six promising approaches to civic education (Carnegie Corporation of New York & CIRCLE, 2003). The report was well received, but its vision of renewed civic education never came to be, largely because of bad timing.

In 2003, U.S. schools were beginning to implement changes required by the No Child Left Behind (NCLB) Act of 2001. NCLB focused on improving student performance in mathematics and reading and put in place an accountability system for schools that did not perform well. The results for civic education were catastrophic. According to Hansen et al. (2018):

> [There was] a net decrease in social studies instruction time for grades one to six over the next two decades. This was especially true in struggling school districts who reallocated instructional time and poured resources into meeting these new math and literacy standards (as cited in Driscoll & McCusker, 2020).

We believe that the failure to reform civic education and the erosion of instruction in civic education are contributing factors to the civic dysfunction and cynicism toward government that exist today. The creation of a modern vision for civic education is the answer.

We need to provide students with access to the mechanisms of democracy and the skills to navigate them. Not doing so leaves them disadvantaged in the system with harmful long-term effects such as low voter participation and a lack of understanding on how to address their grievances.

As educators (and authors) who have spent most of our lives in the classroom, we are aware of the challenges that rethinking civic education presents. As government teachers who have navigated the political minefield of discussing current events in increasingly partisan times, we understand that some might be inclined to stay away from a topic that could be seen as a hot potato. However, the need for change is pressing, the path for achieving it is clear, and the potential benefits for students are profound.

We cannot hope to be part of a society that values *active citizens* if we do not give students access to the mechanisms of government in civic education programs. We can't develop active citizens if civic education does not include performing real acts of citizenship. Having students participate in civic engagement through appropriate avenues is incredibly important. We have a responsibility to ensure students understand how to enact change through democratic processes that respect democratic institutions. They should be armed with a greater, more nuanced understanding of how to accomplish this.

About This Book

This book has three parts. Part 1 (chapters 1 and 2) examines the state of civic education. Before we can reimagine civic education, we must look at a snapshot of how civics classrooms work. We explore the purpose of civic education and how varying interpretations of what it means to be a "good citizen" have impacted the design of civic education programs. What strategies do teachers rely on the most, how effective are they, and what might be improved? The most effective strategies for civic education are clear, but they have not gained traction in classrooms.

In part 2 (chapters 3–6), we discuss the power of authentic experiences, take a deep look at proven practices, and provide practical strategies for implementing them. We examine how civic life has evolved and ways that we can better prepare students for its demands. Civil discourse takes place in entirely new ways, and students don't need to wait until they are of voting age to participate. We discuss how this cultural shift affects how we approach civic education and explore the power and potential of games and gamification in civic education as well as tools and resources to leverage along the way.

Part 3 (chapters 7–10) focuses on the classroom and answers the question, What does modern, updated civic education look like in practice? We will look at how to develop a vision and design for transformative civic education programs, examine the best time to start teaching students about civics, and look at how district leaders can ensure teachers have what they need to make that vision a reality. We also discuss how to move civic education from the social studies curriculum so *all* teachers are a part of teaching civic values. Finally, we explore how to gauge the quality and impact of your civic education program.

Civic education is an equity issue for 21st century students. Young citizens need to jump into the pool of democracy and practice swimming its waters. The evidence shows that creating a strong program of participatory citizenship in schools has a dramatic effect on future participation in not just voting, but all other forms of civic engagement. These programs empower students to participate and practice exercising their voice.

Civic education should give students the keys to the kingdom—or in this case, the democracy.

PART 1

THE STATE OF CIVIC EDUCATION

Chapter 1

HOW SCHOOLS PROVIDE CIVIC EDUCATION

If looking back on the events of 2020 and 2021 (protests, insurrection, the COVID-19 pandemic, and so on) has taught us anything, it is that a nuanced understanding of the U.S. Constitution is necessary to participate in modern civic dialogue, and we need to consider what can be done to ensure we are more informed when faced with future crises. Constitutional scholar Jeffrey Rosen explains that we are living in unprecedented times (CBS News, 2021). Rosen is the president of the National Constitution Center, whose website (https://constitutioncenter.org) has been popular as a source of constitutional answers. When asked in a CBS news interview to comment on the popularity of the website, he struck a somber tone.

> There's no doubt that we are in a crisis of civic education. . . . The framers knew that the consequences of constitutional ignorance and being guided by passion rather than reason were armed mobs. Well, we just saw that they were right about that. (Rosen, as cited in CBS News, 2021)

According to the Annenberg Foundation, in 2019, only 29 percent of Americans could name all three branches of government, and 25 percent couldn't name even one (Annenberg Public Policy Center, 2021). Consider how this may have contributed to divisions in the United States following the 2020 presidential election, as citizens collectively tried to navigate events that, to be truly understood, required knowledge of the electoral college, federalism, Article 1 of the U.S. Constitution, Senate and House rules and procedures, the 14th and 25th amendments, and the U.S. census. In the 2020 U.S. presidential election, 158,383,403 people voted (Federal Election Commission, n.d.). If the Annenberg Public Policy Center is correct, only roughly 46 million of them knew all three branches of government, and 40 million couldn't name a single one. In 2021, 56 percent of Americans could name all three branches due to the wall-to-wall news coverage (Annenberg Public Policy Center, 2021). Ideally, citizens in the United States and other democratic societies around the world would possess essential knowledge about their government and its functions *before* they face a crisis where it is crucial to understanding the events that are unfolding around them.

Modern Civic Engagement

When male Roman citizens came of age during the classical age, they went to the forum in Rome and received the robes of a citizen, which they had to wear whenever they participated at the forum. The bar for becoming a citizen was high, and while there was hope that a person might someday be granted citizenship, it was rare (Johnston, 1957).

Now, young people are more likely to begin participating in civic discourse on their phones using social media while sitting on the couch. Yet, democratic systems for preparing citizens to participate in civic discourse have not caught up to the trend. Schools are still waiting until students are very close to voting age, in most cases, before they teach students the skills necessary to be effective citizens. The need for civic education exists well before they take a government class or pass the U.S. Constitution test commonly given in high school—because students are exposed to political conversations from the moment they begin to use social media apps. Many issues in a democracy affect young people, and while they gain the right to vote at age eighteen in many countries, they do not have to wait until then to become engaged in addressing these issues.

Conversely, *civic deserts* are a growing issue in the United States and elsewhere around the world. These are places where there is little or no opportunity for people to meet and discuss the issues and problems that they face. An estimated 60 percent of rural and 30 percent of urban and suburban Americans perceive their own communities to be civic deserts (Atwell, Bridgeland, & Levine, 2017). Effective civic education can help students see the opportunities that exist in their communities and teach them the skills to participate once they find them.

The Making of Good Citizens

So, what makes someone a good citizen of a democratic society? If our goal is to produce good citizens, it is important to clarify what success looks like. In his book *The Good Citizen: A History of American Civic Life*, Michael Schudson (1998) describes the evolution of American thinking on citizenship. In the 18th century, a model citizen was one who deferred to the political authority of the local aristocracy. By the 19th century, a model citizen was one who was loyal to his or her political party. The Progressive Era of the early 1900s redefined good citizens as those who educated themselves to be informed decision makers. By the late 20th century, a new vision had emerged—good citizens were those who joined with others to fight for their rights. If we want to produce good citizens, we must first acknowledge that this is a moving target.

In the seminal study "What Kind of Citizen? The Politics of Educating for Democracy" (2004), researchers Joel Westheimer and Joseph Kahne identify three views of citizenship that are active in U.S. education: the personally responsible citizen, the participatory citizen, and the justice-oriented citizen (see table 1.1).

Table 1.1: Kinds of Citizens

	Personally Responsible Citizen	**Participatory Citizen**	**Justice-Oriented Citizen**
Description	• Acts responsibly in his or her community • Works and pays taxes • Obeys laws • Recycles, gives blood • Volunteers to lend a hand in times of crisis	• Active member of community organizations or improvement efforts • Organizes community efforts to care for those in need, promote economic development, or clean up environment • Knows how government agencies work • Knows strategies for accomplishing collective tasks	• Critically assesses social, political, and economic structures to see beyond surface causes • Seeks out and addresses areas of injustice • Knows about social movements and how to effect systemic change

continued →

	Personally Responsible Citizen	**Participatory Citizen**	**Justice-Oriented Citizen**
Sample Action	• Contributes food to a food drive	• Helps to organize a food drive	• Explores why people are hungry and acts to solve root causes
Core Assumptions	• To solve social problems and improve society, citizens must have good character; they must be honest, responsible, and law-abiding members of the community.	• To solve social problems and improve society, citizens must actively participate and take leadership positions within established systems and community structures.	• To solve social problems and improve society, citizens must question and change established systems and structures when they reproduce patterns of injustice over time.

Source: *Westheimer & Kahne, 2004, pp. 239–240.*

The first and most prominent view is that of the *personally responsible citizen*. This view defines good citizenship through the lens of personal behavior and character. Self-disciplined and compassionate, personally responsible citizens model integrity. The second, far less common view, the participatory citizen, is characterized by action. These citizens are active in their community and more broadly in state and national issues. More than just contributing to a cause, they are likely to lead one. Least common of all is the view of the justice-oriented citizen. This citizen would feel obliged to learn about the forces and conditions that create injustice—then, having identified them, would seek to change them in order in the name of a more just society.

After analyzing the work of Schudson (1998) and Westheimer and Kahne (2004), professor Howard Budin, co-founder of the Center for Technology and School Change, outlined his own definition of democracy and citizenship. The strength of his vision lies in how he ties not only the skills required for democratic citizenship, but also the conditions that foster the skills.

> First, democracy is not something that happens only occasionally or at certain times of the year. Rather, it is, or should be, continuous and ongoing. Thus, democracy is, or should be, an integral part of our everyday lives.
>
> Second, schooling is not just practice for life but is part of life, and the skills and dispositions we learn in school should be those we continue to use as adults.
>
> Third, the heart of democratic action is collaborative decision making. One of the key roles of democratic citizens is to make decisions with their fellow

citizens to improve their lives and the life of the community or nation. Voting is one type of decision, but life is filled with situations that need to be addressed.

Fourth, decision making entails critical thinking and problem solving, as part of real situations in which there are problems to be solved.

Fifth, problems are solved not by individuals in isolation, but through communication and collaboration with others. Thus, problem solving is a social activity.

Sixth, groups solve problems through the process of deliberation. Deliberation produces "a decision to take a particular course of action," and it involves "forging that decision together, reasoning together, generating and considering alternatives together."

Seventh, deliberate decision making requires that all involved have access to all the information they need, and have the skills to analyze information in order to think through problems.

Eighth, to be truly effective, deliberation needs a diversity of viewpoints and opinions, to help in learning to understand other perspectives. Deliberation is a "public-building" activity, and a public must include diverse points of view. (H. Budin, personal communication, August 12, 2011)

Although the views on what make a good democratic citizen may vary, it's important that people are informed and educated about how to be active and productive in the democratic system. Let's examine how people actually learn about civics and how the past can inform the future.

Traditional Civics Instruction

If you take a moment to reflect on how you learned about government, chances are it did not change much from the classes your parents and grandparents took. It is likely that your class consisted of mostly classroom instruction provided by your teacher that aimed to help you pass a required U.S. Constitution test. The classroom instruction probably took the form of information delivery, and the test itself, more likely than not, was derived from or similar to the U.S. citizenship test given to prospective citizens during the naturalization process. This is what civic education is in the United States.

The 2018 Brown Center Report on American Education: How Well Are American Students Learning? (Hansen et al., 2018) offers a revealing look at classroom practice and how civic education classes are conducted. The report notes that the opportunity to participate actively in government processes is extremely rare across the United States, "while discussion and knowledge-building components of civic education appear common across states" (Hansen et al., 2018, p. 16). Also common is the practice of discussing current events, typically led by the teacher explaining news stories of the day. More participatory practices, such as service learning, are extremely rare.

Now as in the past, most students still engage in civic education programs far more through lecture and classroom discussion than through authentic participation in civic life. It is fair to say that not only is this what civic education looks like, it's what we *expect* it to be. It will take a concerted effort to change this, and there are some challenges that we must overcome to do so.

In their book *Tinkering Toward Utopia*, David Tyack and Larry Cuban (1995) refer to the challenge that people believe schooling should look like what it was when they were young as *the grammar of schooling*. This concept suggests that some things are so ingrained in schools that they become widely accepted and remain relatively unquestioned (for example, the way time is allocated, the work that students are asked to do, the system of grading, or in this case, the way that schools and teachers envision classroom instruction in civics). Making the changes we suggest later in this book requires skill-based civic education that values experience and direct participation.

Another challenge that must be overcome is the legacy of the No Child Left Behind Act of 2001. This law did not specifically or directly aim to harm civic education but was nonetheless responsible for a decades-long degradation.

Shortly after the passage of NCLB, in 2003, the Carnegie Corporation of New York and CIRCLE published *The Civic Mission of Schools*. Written in collaboration with a broad spectrum of experts, researchers, and scholars, this seminal work discusses what civic education in America's classrooms should become (Carnegie Corporation of New York & CIRCLE, 2003). It crafted a vision of a richer, more meaningful approach to civic education in the United States.

As noted earlier, the report describes a trend toward cynical views of government institutions and civic engagement among U.S. students and society. With strong echoes of Robert D. Putnam's (1995) "Bowling Alone: America's Declining Social Capital," *The Civic Mission of Schools* (Carnegie Corporation of New York & CIRCLE, 2003) outlines challenging trends in society and notes the potential of schools to heroically influence change and provide high-quality civic education programs. However, this potential was never reached; NCLB (2002) saw to that.

Under NCLB (2002), schools across the United States moved to increase instruction in literacy, mathematics, and science, the subjects that would be the focus of high-stakes testing (Hansen et al., 2018). This led to a stifling of change in civic education practices and began the erosion of the instructional time dedicated to social studies at all levels. Schools adjusted their instructional priorities to increase time for reading, writing, mathematics, and science. At the same time, social studies classrooms were called on to increase their focus on reading and writing instruction and teaching effective testing practices. As a result, the call for change made in

The Civic Mission of Schools (Carnegie Corporation of New York & CIRCLE, 2003) went largely unheeded.

NCLB's focus on science, technology, engineering, and mathematics (STEM) and English language arts (ELA) also adversely affected federal funding for civic education. In the early 2000s, the U.S. government still regularly spent $40 million a year on civic education. By 2010, the U.S. government was spending $3 billion a year on STEM while the federal funding for civic education had fallen to just $4 million per year. Ted McConnell, the executive director of the campaign for the Civic Mission of Schools, put this in perspective: "That's $54 per school child in this country [for STEM] as opposed to the very paltry amount of about five cents per student spent on civics" (Adams, 2019).

By 2016, the fractured and polarized nature of modern politics had become a crisis, and there was a renewed interest that focused attention on the topic of civic education again. For some, the acrimony and hostility among not just elected officials but the American populace were a *Sputnik* moment for civic education that demanded immediate action.

Civic Education Requirements

As of 2018, only nine states require a full year of civic education, while thirty-one states require half a year. Nine states have no civics requirement at all. Sixteen states require that students pass a civics exam to graduate from high school, but the majority of these programs and tests is modeled after the U.S. Citizenship and Immigration Services Naturalization Test, which emphasizes factual information over the skills and dispositions required to be an informed citizen (Shapiro & Brown, 2018).

Florida was an early adopter of civic education reform. This reform began in 2010 with the passage of a law that created a mandatory middle school civics program, but also included funding for the development of model civics lessons and professional development for teachers. In the wake of the political campaigns for the 2016 election, many states began to bolster civic education programs. Illinois (in 2015) and Massachusetts (in 2018) followed the trend by also adding a requirement for middle and high school civics course, but went a step further by also writing aspects of proven practices into law, especially as it relates to service learning, discussion of current and controversial issues, and media literacy (Sawchuk, 2019a). Rather than the delivery of factual information, these strategies ask students to actively engage with the government, to explore and develop their own political beliefs and values, and to be reflective and aware of the sources of information that they use to become educated. This is a positive development. Although these proven practices have been at the core of civic education research for years, and despite evidence demonstrating that when they are in place, students' civic participation increases, these practices are still not a dominant part of the typical classroom. Unfortunately, civic education for most students still takes place through lecture rather than participation (Hansen et al., 2018).

Table 1.2 shows U.S. civic education requirements, by state. (Note that the mean scores on the U.S. government advanced placement [AP] exam are based on a scale of 1 to 5, with 1 being worst and 5 being best.)

Table 1.2: State-by-State Civics Requirements

\multicolumn{7}{c}{**Civic Education Measures**}

\multicolumn{7}{c}{**Civic Education Requirements for All High Schools, by State**}

State	**Requires Civics Course**	**Length of Course (in Years)**	**Full Curriculum***	**Requires Community Service**	**Mean Score on the U.S. Government AP Exam**	**Requires Civics Exam to Graduate**
Alabama	✓	0.5	✓	No	2.27	✓
Alaska		0		No	2.72	
Arizona	✓	0.5	✓	No	2.73	✓
Arkansas	✓	0.5	✓	Provides credit	2.25	✓
California	✓	0.5	✓	No	2.53	
Colorado	✓	1	✓	No	2.74	
Connecticut	✓	0.5	✓	Provides credit	3.07	
Delaware		0		Provides credit	2.8	
District of Columbia	✓	1	✓	Required	2.33	
Florida	✓	0.5		Provides credit	2.32	****
Georgia	✓	0.5	✓	Provides credit	2.64	
Hawaii	✓	1	✓	Provides credit	2.68	
Idaho	✓	1	✓	No	2.99	✓

Illinois	☑	0.5	☑	Provides credit	2.69	
Indiana	☑	0.5	☑	Provides credit	2.53	
Iowa	☑	0.5		No	2.85	
Kansas	☑	1	☑	No	2.89	
Kentucky		0		No	2.51	☑
Louisiana	☑	0.5	☑	No	2.4	☑
Maine	☑	0.5		No	2.76	
Maryland	☑	1	☑	Required	2.92	
Massachusetts	☑	0.5		No	2.88	
Michigan	☑	0.5	☑	No	2.81	
Minnesota	☑	0.5		Provides credit	3.1	☑
Mississippi	☑	0.5	☑	No	1.88	
Missouri	☑	0.5		Provides credit	2.77	☑
Montana		0		No	2.77	
Nebraska		0		No	2.57	
Nevada	☑	1	☑	Provides credit	2.33	
New Hampshire	☑	0.5	☑	Provides credit	3.14	☑
New Jersey		0		Provides credit	3.09	
New Mexico	☑	0.5		Provides credit	1.96	
New York	☑	0.5		No	2.74	
North Carolina	☑	1		No	2.68	....
North Dakota	☑	0.5	☑	Provides credit	2.80	☑
Ohio	☑	0.5	☑	Provides credit	2.79	
Oklahoma	☑	0.5	☑	Provides credit	2.57	

continued →

State	Requires Civics Course	Length of Course (in Years)	Full Curriculum*	Requires Community Service	Mean Score on the U.S. Government AP Exam	Requires Civics Exam to Graduate
Oregon		0		Provides credit	2.77	
Pennsylvania	✓	0.5	✓	No	2.87	
Rhode Island		0		No	2.99	
South Carolina	✓	0.5	✓	No	2.87	✓
South Dakota	✓	0.5	✓	Provides credit	2.96	
Tennessee	✓	0.5	✓	Provides credit	2.65	✓
Texas	✓	0.5	✓	Provides credit	2.20	
Utah	✓	0.5	✓	No	2.99	✓
Vermont		0		No	3.41	✓
Virginia	✓	1		No	3.03	
Washington		0	✓	Provides credit	2.94	
West Virginia	✓	1	✓	Provides credit	2.30	
Wisconsin** ***	✓	0.5		No	2.95	✓
Wyoming	✓	0.5	✓	No	2.74	✓

* "Full curriculum" includes course materials that cover "Explanation/Comparison of Democracy," "Constitution & Bill of Rights," and "Public Participation," as well as information on state and local voting rules.

**Correction, May 10, 2018: This [table has been] updated to accurately present Wisconsin's curriculum requirements.

***Correction, June 6, 2018: This [table] has been updated to reflect the fact that Wisconsin has a civic education requirement.

****Correction, December 19, 2019: This [table] has been updated to clarify that Florida does not have a civics exam requirement in high school.

Source: Shapiro & Brown, 2018. This material was published by the Center for American Progress (www.americanprogress.org).

The controversy surrounding the 2020 U.S. presidential election further illustrates that something must be done to improve civic education. In her article "We Were Warned," Beth R. Holland (2021) argues that the response to the election's results shouldn't be surprising since that is what is expected when "our education system has failed to prepare the majority of citizens for active participation in a democratic society."

And yet, we are extremely hopeful. There is a path forward, and we believe that schools are heroically positioned to address this need. Even better, there is abundant research on how to do it. As we discuss in chapter 2 (page 21), we know what we need to do.

The problem is, despite the volume of evidence and research and despite the work done by organizations like the Center for Information and Research on Civic Learning and Engagement, Civic Mission of Schools, and Center for Civic Education, we have not done enough to enact these changes in a meaningful way. There is a lack of deep and meaningful understanding of what these strategies for improving civic education are and a general lack of examples of what they look like in practice. We intend to demonstrate both.

Conclusion

In this chapter, we examined the state of civic education and how civic participation has changed. We examined different views of what it means to be a good citizen and then explored traditional civic education instruction and what it looks like in schools across the United States and other democratic societies. In chapter 2, we will explore how civic education *should* look and the strategies that research shows could transform how students learn about participating in a democracy.

Key Takeaways for How Schools Provide Civic Education

Following are some key takeaways from this chapter on how schools provide civic education.

- ▸ Research shows that most Americans lack a basic understanding of the structure of government, the importance of the separation of powers, and what rights are specifically guaranteed in the U.S. Constitution.

- ▸ Students are using social media to participate in civic discourse at a young age and do not wait, as was typical in the past, until they are of voting age to engage in the process. As a result, the need for civic education exists well before students take their U.S. Constitution test, typically given in high school.

- ▸ Large numbers of students live in civic deserts where they do not have the opportunity to meet and discuss the problems they face or learn how to access the mechanisms of democracy. Effective civic education is crucial in preparing students in these areas to be citizens.

- Traditional civics instruction typically took the form of a lecture, and the students' role was to receive information. This remains largely true today; although we have research that shows how to best reform civic education, little has been done to enact change.
- Schools are in a position to address the problem of civic education, but as yet they largely have not done so, and there are still states with no formal requirement for civic education.

Chapter 2

WHAT WORKS IN CIVIC EDUCATION

Before diving into best practices in civic education, it is worth starting with the end goal in mind. What are we hoping to achieve? What are the overarching goals of civic education? How would we actually know if we are providing students with an effective civic education experience? Is there even general agreement regarding what aspects of civic education should be the focus of our attention, resources, and policy reforms?

As expected, when considering such a vast patchwork of independent civic education programs, research institutes, and school systems, the answer to what effective civics looks like varies. Despite this, there is general consensus around several themes.

A powerful 2019 study conducted an analysis of education policies from all fifty states in the United States, interviewed more than one hundred experts in the field, and interacted with forty civic education foundations; it found that "almost everyone we interviewed believes that an ideal system of civic education should be designed to produce citizens who are well-informed, productively engaged in working for the common good and hopeful about our democracy" (Red & Blue Works, 2019, p. 4). Similar sentiments exist in the Canadian education system, evident by a 2019 report that "calls on Canada and the provinces to take a more coordinated and sustained approach to building civic literacy across generations" (People for Education, 2019).

Despite the similarity of these shared viewpoints regarding the importance of civic literacy, breaking down each of the bigger concepts is needed to understand more clearly what knowledge and skills translate to effective civic education.

Although many organizations have a framework of civic learning competencies, one that stands out as an effective balance of scope and specificity comes from the Democratic Knowledge Project (n.d.), a K–12 and college-level civic education provider based at Harvard University. It outlines the following four dimensions of civic learning and expression as civic knowledge, civic skills, civic dispositions, and civic capacities.

1. **Civic knowledge:** An understanding of government structure, government processes, relevant social studies knowledge and concepts, and American history and political thought in a global context
2. **Civic skills:** Competencies in the use of one's voice, including basic writing, speaking, and listening skills and skills of research, investigation, and critical thinking; competencies in the use of practices of democratic coordination, political institutions, and media literacy
3. **Civic dispositions:** Attitudes important in a democracy, such as a sense of civic duty, sense of efficacy, concern for the welfare of others, and commitment to trustworthiness and bridge-building
4. **Civic capacities:** Access to networks, opportunities to participate, and other forms of social capital that promote civic agency (Democratic Knowledge Project, n.d.)

A 2019 Canadian study by the Samara Centre for Democracy developed a similar framework for effective civic literacy. The four dimensions of civic literacy include (1) institutional knowledge, (2) political ability, (3) topical knowledge, and (4) media literacy (Samara Centre for Democracy, 2019). Both of these organizations conclude that most civic education has historically focused on the domain of civic and institutional knowledge. Many of the instructional shifts described in the next section are aimed at skills, dispositions, and capacities. This is where much of the more difficult yet exciting and impactful work lies. This is how students go from *learning* about being an informed citizen to *living* as an informed citizen engaged as a member of a democratic society. Let's examine the shifts in practice necessary to achieve these lofty goals.

The Promise and Potential of Schools

As noted in the previous chapter, most civics instruction, when provided at all, focuses primarily on traditional approaches involving large-group instruction via lecture or classroom discussion. However, emerging research consistently calls for a shift in practices that lead to improved civic education outcomes. When paired with these effective teaching practices, educational technologies have the power to amplify the impact of student experiences. We will now take a closer look at these research-based changes in practice and the necessary instructional design shifts needed to enhance civic education for all students. In part 2 (page 31) of the book, we explore implementation of these practices in greater detail.

The Civic Mission of Schools (Carnegie Corporation of New York & CIRCLE, 2003) outlines a series of key practices that exemplify high-quality civic education. The report calls for a more comprehensive and authentic student experience and highlights the promise and potential of schools to help reverse the trend toward cynicism and disengagement. Not only could schools help create a more informed and engaged citizenry, but they could also be leveraged to help address systemic inequalities in the quality of civic learning among disadvantaged communities.

In *Guardian of Democracy* (Gould, Jamieson, Levine, McConnell, & Smith, 2011), the authors, sensing that initial call to action in *The Civic Mission of Schools* (Carnegie Corporation of New York & CIRCLE, 2003) fell on deaf ears, again sounded the alarm. Along with another in-depth discussion of the promising practices of civic education, they warned that "the country shortchanges the civic mission of its schools at its peril" (Gould et al., 2011, p. 4).

So, what are some of these best practices? Gould and colleagues (2011) outline the following.

▸ **Offer explicit instruction in government, history, economics, law, and democracy:** In these courses, or parts of the curriculum, students must engage in rich discussions of current events and related civic issues, especially topics that are relevant and meaningful to them.

▸ **Provide opportunities for students to engage in simulations of democratic processes, whether through role-playing activities or virtual experiences:** This understanding of civic concepts and current events can then be further enriched in school programs that extend outside learning of the classroom. One way is to provide students with opportunities to apply their understanding through authentic experiences in the local community, also described as service learning. You also can achieve this through extracurricular activities that encourage engagement in the local community and establish school government programs that model democratic principles within the school community.

A lot has changed in the world since the updated *Civic Mission* report in 2011. The study, *The Republic Is (Still) at Risk—and Civics Is Part of the Solution* (Levine & Kawashima-Ginsberg, 2017), reinforces the need for six proven practices of civic education as a cornerstone of education.

1. Schools must devote time and space in the curriculum to teach full courses on civics and related topics. A primary reason for this is to provide opportunities for students to engage more fully in the other five practices.
2. Students must engage in deliberation and well-designed class discussions around current events and controversial issues of our time.
3. Students should have opportunities to engage in service learning, particularly those that connect community service to the academic topics core to the class.
4. Educators should enable and encourage students to engage in their own student-led associations that have high degrees of autonomy, participation, and shared purpose.
5. Schools must create conditions for students to have a voice in their school, particularly related to climate and policies that impact the student body.
6. Effective civic education programs provide ample, high-quality simulations of adult civic roles. This can include elections, mock trials, and online games and simulations.

Along with these six best practices, the study (Levine & Kawashima-Ginsberg, 2017) calls for educators to consider four complementary practices in light of changes in civic life and public education in general.

1. **High-quality news media literacy:** Students must have access to high-quality news media literacy education. The rapid evolution of the news and social media industries continues to change the way citizens access information and engage in civil life, and the ability to do so effectively is increasingly vital to modern citizenship.
2. **Specific focus on action civics**: The authors also advocate for more specific focus on what they call *action civics*. Action civics goes beyond most service learning projects, as the goal is not only to have students identify and address issues in the community but to do so by considering influencing institutional policies as part of their proposed solution. (We discuss action civics and implementation strategies in more detail in chapter 3, page 33.)

3. **Increased focus on social-emotional learning (SEL):** Another new area of focus is on SEL, which has garnered attention in school districts across the United States (Collaborative for Academic, Social, and Emotional Learning [CASEL], 2021). Social-emotional learning has also become a point of emphasis in provinces across Canada, demonstrated by dedicated resource pages for SEL skills and mental health in schools (Ontario Ministry of Education, 2021). The connection here is that schools that focus on SEL enhance students' social-emotional skills, which in turn put them in a better position to "be more ethical and effective citizens" (Levine & Kawashima-Ginsberg, 2017, p. 5). Conversely, having students engage in authentic civic education experiences can enhance SEL skills as well.

4. **School climate reform:** The last recommendation involves what the authors term *school climate reform*, which aims squarely at equity issues that persist across the American school system. For example, research shows that higher levels of school suspension rates result in lower voting and volunteering rates for those students later in life (Kupchik & Catlaw, 2015). Promising research points to schools that effectively enact restorative justice and related approaches "show promise for enhancing schools' civic outcomes" (Levine & Kawashima-Ginsberg, 2017, p. 5).

Implementation Strategies for Best Practices in Civic Education

Following are examples of how you can implement each of the best practices listed on pages 24–25. We will explore several of these best practices in much greater depth with classroom examples throughout part 2 (page 31).

Courses on Civics, Government, Law, and Related Topics

Designated classes in civics and related subjects provide students with quality opportunities to apply each of the best practices that follow. They also provide educators that teach these subjects with the time and training to implement civic education with greater effectiveness.

For example: Massachusetts's social studies curriculum outlines a renewed mission for civic life in a democracy, which requires all grade 8 students to take a course solely focused on U.S. and Massachusetts government and civic life. Throughout the course, students learn about the philosophical foundations of the U.S. political system, rights and responsibilities of citizens, and news media literacy, and will demonstrate civic knowledge, skills, and dispositions (Massachusetts Department of

Elementary and Secondary Education, 2020). The Ontario Ministry of Education (2013) curriculum guide also includes specific civics instruction as a core part of their grades 9–10 curriculum on Canadian and world studies. According to the curricular progressions, the grade 10 civics course provides "numerous opportunities for students to explore the four elements of the citizenship education framework: identity, attributes, structures, and active participation" (Ontario Ministry of Education, 2013).

Deliberations of Current, Controversial Issues

Teachers mindfully craft learning experiences that involve rich dialogue, discussion, and debate on civics-related topics. They value, consistently practice, and accurately assess the skills and dispositions needed to effectively engage in academic discourse.

For example: In a unit on civil rights, teachers can leverage the Flipgrid platform (info.flipgrid.com) to present students with a discussion prompt that sparks asynchronous video discussion by students. These video-based discussion threads can then translate into deeper live conversations during class in a larger group. This approach also hones students' ability to engage in dialogue through digital means, a form of democratic participation that is becoming increasingly popular across the world. A 2020 UNICEF study concluded that a growing percentage of youth worldwide is "taking to digital spaces to develop their civic identities and express political stances in creative ways, claiming agency that may not be afforded to them in traditional civic spaces" (UNICEF Office of Global Insight and Policy, 2020).

Service Learning

Service learning falls under the umbrella of "community engagement pedagogies [that] integrate meaningful community services with instruction and reflection to enrich the learning experience, teach civic responsibility, and strengthen communities" (Bandy, 2011). It is typically integrated into classrooms through projects that focus on applying course content and skills to community-based activities.

For example: The Service Learning Project (SLP) in Brooklyn, New York, provides school-day and after-school programs that create "opportunities for . . . youth to become active citizens in their schools and communities" (Vander Ark & Leibtag, 2021, p. 54). Middle school students in one of the SLP partnership schools recently focused their service learning project on voter education and turnout in New York City. After learning that only 14 percent of registered voters participated in local elections, they created and published a comprehensive NYC Voter Guide website that includes "information about how to vote, the benefits of ranked choice voting and the roles and responsibilities of various local elected officials" (Service Learning Project, 2022).

Student Voice in Schools

As previously described in the *Guardian of Democracy* (Gould et al., 2011) report, research suggests that "giving students more opportunities to participate in the management of their own classrooms and schools builds their civic skills and attitudes." Providing structures for students to express their views within the school environment, particularly regarding ways to improve their school community, is an effective way to model effective democratic practices and dispositions.

For example: Creating the space and support for student government is one of the most promising practices related to student voice in schools. Although they can come in many forms, the National Association of Student Councils recommends that school programs include the following four components: "activities must be structured, students must make a substantial time commitment to activities, activities must engage student interest, and students' decisions must have real effects" (Gould et al., 2011).

Simulations of Adult Civic Roles

To create simulations, teachers can leverage online simulations and games that place students in civic roles related to voting, public advocacy, defending civil rights, and more.

For example: Teachers can use the iCivics platform (www.icivics.org) to engage students in a wide range of curriculum-aligned online simulations of democratic engagement. In Do I Have a Right? (iCivics, n.d.c), students assume the role of a founding member of a firm specializing in constitutional law. Throughout the game, students must recognize if the rights of potential clients have been violated, and if so, which amendment (or collection of amendments) protect the rights that were allegedly violated. In the Executive Command (iCivics, n.d.d) simulation, students assume the role of a U.S. president tasked with setting and enacting an agenda, all the while responding to emerging challenges throughout the four-year presidential term.

High-Quality News Media Literacy Education

For this activity, students engage in an in-depth study of news media and the various ways to assess the validity of sources. They should pay careful attention to the emerging and evolving industry that purposefully develops and propagates false information for profit and learn how to detect that content.

For example: Leveraging the online Checkology platform (https://get.checkology.org) by the News Literacy Project, educators can assign students a variety of lessons that help hone their skills when navigating the world of online information and news media. More specifically, students "identify credible information, seek out reliable sources, and apply critical thinking skills to separate fact-based content from falsehoods" (Checkology, n.d.b). In the InfoZones lesson (https://get.checkology.org/lesson/infozones), students analyze information and sort it into categories such as news, entertainment, advertising, and propaganda. In the Democracy's Watchdog lesson (https://get.checkology.org/lesson/democracys-watchdog), students investigate a series of documents that highlight the historical role of the free press in the United States. The Conspiratorial Thinking lesson (https://get.checkology.org/lesson/conspiratorial-thinking) further helps students understand the powerful effect conspiracy theories can have on people, along with the cognitive science research that explains why they are often tricked by them.

Specific Focus on Action Civics

For action civics, students engage in research around issues and challenges facing their community. Based on the research, students develop public policy solutions and propose them to officials who could implement them at the appropriate level of government.

For example: As part of the Generation Citizen (https://generationcitizen.org) action civics program, a group of New York City public school students researched the debate around monuments and their degree of representation of all Americans. After researching the issue, along with a study of related historical eras, students developed a public policy proposal to build memorials of African American abolitionists. The project culminated with students proposing their ideas during a visit to the mayor's office to explore further actions.

Increased Focus on Social-Emotional Learning

According to the Collaborative for Academic, Social, and Emotional Learning (CASEL, 2022a), social-emotional learning is:

> The process through which all young people and adults acquire and apply the knowledge, skills, and attitudes to develop healthy identities, manage emotions and achieve personal and collective goals, feel and show empathy for others, establish and maintain supportive relationships, and make responsible and caring decisions.

As schools embrace and commit to a focus on social-emotional learning (SEL), it is becoming evident that effective civics instruction can help bolster students' SEL competencies. In *The Republic Is (Still) at Risk* (Levine & Kawashina-Ginsberg, 2017), the authors make the case that "students with better socioemotional skills are likely to be more ethical and effective citizens, and experiences with civic learning can boost SEL outcomes."

For example: When engaged in civic learning, students develop a range of social and emotional skills. One example is when students research issues related to their school and communities, and they tend to develop self- and social awareness. When students engage in collaborative action civics projects, the process of developing a public policy solution fosters self-management, relationship skills, and responsible decision making (CASEL, 2022a).

School Climate Reform

Although school climate reform and civic education may not at first seem like complementary fields of research, there is an alarming connection between poor school climate and low civic participation rates (Levine & Kawashima-Ginsberg, 2017). Also, for many of the previously noted practices to flourish, such as student voice and deliberation of controversial issues, a healthy school climate serves as the foundation for these civic learning experiences.

For example: Approaches aimed at enhancing student climate, such as restorative practices, show promise for enhancing schools' civic outcomes (Levine & Kawashima-Ginsberg, 2017). Restorative practices refer to disciplinary strategies that focus on developing healthy in-school relationships and experiences, as opposed to zero-tolerance policies that focus on removing students from the school. A Learning Policy Institute report (Kleven, 2021) highlights studies that "suggest a link between restorative approaches and improved school climate outcomes, including increased levels of student connectedness, improved relationships between students and teachers, and improved perceptions of school climate."

Conclusion

In part 1, we discussed the current state of civics instruction, why we need to refocus our efforts on civic education, and what constitutes best practices in this field. Chapter 2 also provided examples of these practices in action. In part 2, we shift to an in-depth exploration of three high-leverage practices: authentic action civics projects, civil discourse, quality news media literacy instruction, and engagement through digital games and competitions.

Key Takeaways for What Works in Civic Education

Following are key takeaways from this chapter on what works in civic education.

- Despite the wide array of government agencies, school systems, research institutes, and education programs, a general consensus emerges regarding the goals of effective civic education. Students must be well-informed about their system of government, its founding ideals, and current issues facing their communities. They must also have the knowledge and skills necessary to be active and engaged participants in our democratic society. Finally, students will develop strong civic dispositions such as a sense of civic duty and concern for the welfare of others.

- Schools play a vital role in achieving these goals. Best practices in effective civic education in schools include the devotion of time in the curriculum to teach civics, engaging students in discussions of current events and controversial issues, participating in service learning opportunities, fostering student-led associations and student voice in decision making, and facilitating simulations of adult civic roles.

- Four complementary practices have recently emerged that amplify the impact of effective civic education programs. This includes implementation of high-quality news media literacy instruction, student engagement in authentic action civics projects, a focus on social-emotional learning to help develop civic dispositions, and school climate initiatives that lay the groundwork for effective participation and collaboration in civics activities.

PART 2

MODERN CIVICS IN ACTION

Chapter 3

THE POWER OF ACTION CIVICS AND AUTHENTIC EXPERIENCES

Before diving into action civics, it helps to define what we mean by a traditional approach to civic education. Most traditional educators tend to focus on systems and structures of government. In the United States, this comes with an in-depth study of the founding fathers, the Constitution, and the Bill of Rights and subsequent amendments. Along with these topics, these teachers tend to revere the United States and its institutions, with a goal to promote a sense of unifying patriotism and civic responsibility (Levine & Kawashima-Ginsberg, 2015).

Although framing this as an either-or scenario oversimplifies it, there are key differences between a traditional approach and action civics. Educators who advocate for action civics tend to encourage students to identify societal problems and design public policy solutions to address them. This approach also encourages students to reach out to public officials and mobilize support for their public policy solutions.

Action civics has significant overlap with other concepts, such as service learning, project-based learning, experiential learning, and others. Despite the overlap, the idea of action civics has gained traction with civic education organizations in a way that weaves these concepts into a more comprehensive approach to teaching civic action (Levine & Kawashima-Ginsberg, 2017). Understanding the founding era, the U.S. Constitution, and other, more traditional concepts is still considered important, but these are the background knowledge and context needed for more essential learning experiences involving civic action.

The idea behind action civics is to learn civics through experiential learning and collective action. Guided by an educator, students develop projects that aim to solve problems in their communities by advocating public policy changes to local leaders (Generation Citizen, n.d.d). A main focus of this approach is tapping into youth expertise and voice to empower students. To do this, action civics also forgoes the traditional focus on national government and instead has students engage on a local level.

Another difference between action civics and traditional approaches is that instead of promoting unity and reverence for democratic institutions, action civics encourages students to view these institutions in a way that can be improved and changed in ways to enhance society and bring people closer to realizing the nation's founding ideals. Some examples of civic actions include engaging in community forums and events, advocating ideas to local officials, and participating in elections and town meetings. From a philosophical standpoint, this approach aligns with more progressive, experiential education (Levine & Kawashima-Ginsberg, 2015).

In this chapter, we unpack the *why* behind action civics and then explore the key components of effective action civics experiences that focus on authentic application of civic knowledge and skills. Following an examination of practical examples of action civics in the classroom, we discuss several key ways to leverage educational technologies to amplify the impact of action civics experiences.

The *Why* of Action Civics

The resurgence of civic education offers an opportunity to redesign traditional approaches that tend to teach students about the political process without providing experiences that help them develop the skills and dispositions to not only participate in but also change and improve the U.S. political system and public policies. As described by researchers Peter Levine and Kei Kawashima-Ginsberg (2015), "Action civics is gaining recognition as an engaging pedagogy that enables students from diverse backgrounds to address relevant and serious community issues through action-oriented pedagogy" (p. 13).

For a variety of reasons, action civics has growing support from educators and civic organizations across the United States. This renewed interest in civic education is also coming during a time of increasing activism by young people across the country since 2016. Some of the core issues of interest to students in 2020 include climate change, immigration, gun regulation, and LGBTQ+ rights (Carney, 2020). Counter to the commonly held belief that youth activism is typically that of passive, online support of issues, a 2018 study by the Center for Information and Research on Civic Learning and Engagement concludes that young people (eighteen to twenty-four years of age) are now three times more likely to attend a demonstration, march, or protest than in 2016 (Center for Information and Research on Civic Learning and Engagement, 2018).

In 2019, a worldwide climate strike, led in part by youth activist Greta Thunberg, involved more than six million participants worldwide, including student-led school walkouts across the United States (Taylor, Watts, & Bartlett, 2019). In 2020, the Black Lives Matter and related protests reached new heights, which included activism on the part of youth across the United States and world (Bennett, 2020). Tapping into these important societal events through an action civics curriculum can help channel this energy and enthusiasm into a deeper understanding of civic knowledge, skills, and dispositions.

Having students practice engaging in this type of authentic civic learning is also aligned to many of the field's proven practices and promising areas of research and classroom practice. Action civics incorporates elements of service learning, deliberation of current controversial issues, and student voice in schools. Students also undoubtedly have the opportunity to learn news media literacy through the action civics process. One of the more promising effects of these authentic experiences is tapping into student engagement and motivation. As discussed in *The Republic Is (Still) at Risk—and Civics Is Part of the Solution* (Levine & Kawashima-Ginsberg, 2017) report, students must do the following:

> Develop an appetite for civic engagement and an identity as effective and engaged citizens. Civic action rarely brings immediate material rewards. Therefore, even if students learn civic knowledge in schools, they will not update, expand, and employ their knowledge as adults unless they *want* to do so. More than with subjects that bring immediate economic benefits, civics requires motivation. (p. 6)

Without motivation and engagement, it is difficult for students to learn anything, never mind the often-complex design and function of government and how to challenge the nature of effectively participating in representative democracy.

Action Civics and Deeper Learning

Looking beyond civic education, there has been an increasing advocacy across the education landscape for *deeper learning* experiences for students. One of the core deeper learning frameworks via the William and Flora Hewlett Foundation (2013) includes competencies such as thinking critically to solve complex problems, working collaboratively, and communicating effectively. For students to develop these skills, they must engage in learning experiences that hone these competencies.

Leading researchers in the field, such as Scott McLeod and Dean Shareski (2018) and Jal Mehta and Sarah Fine (2019), suggest that deeper learning is more common in learning environments characterized by authenticity and real-world learning. For example, authentic work is one of McLeod and Shareski's (2018) *four big shifts* necessary for schools if they are to take the concept of deeper learning seriously. More specifically, authenticity in this context implies "the shift from isolated academic work to environments that provide students opportunities to engage with and contribute to local, national, and international interdisciplinary learning communities" (McLeod & Shareski, 2018, p. 4).

In other words, students are not just learning about a topic in isolation, they are engaging in an age- and skill-level-appropriate version of a real-world scenario. Or, as Mehta and Fine (2019) describe it, students engage in deeper learning when they are "playing the whole game at the junior level" (p. 295). What Mehta and Fine (2019) mean by this is that schools should not focus solely on the content and skills that are a prerequisite to be used in the real world later. They should instead be engaged in learning experiences that replicate those real-world tasks, albeit at a modified level that is appropriate to the students' age and ability level (Mehta & Fine, 2019).

Action civics, as it is typically implemented, aligns well to the types of research-based approaches that lead to deeper student learning. A study on this topic by leading researchers Peter Levine and Kei Kawashima-Ginsberg (2015) suggests that effective civic education supports the development of knowledge, skills, and dispositions that fall under the deeper learning umbrella. They further suggest:

> Students who become involved in experiential civic learning opportunities often have a chance to see tangible results from their efforts to confront meaningful challenges, helping them develop an academic mindset by teaching them the value of hard work and collaboration. (Levine & Kawashima-Ginsberg, 2015, p. 12)

Action civics, therefore, is not just an effective way to teach civic education, but also an approach that promotes deeper student learning of essential skills and dispositions across various academic disciplines. More important, it better prepares them to be informed, active, and engaged citizens in a participatory form of democratic government.

Action Civics Programs

Although there is no single approach to action civics, there are several common elements. In this section, we explore four of the leading action civics programs and parse out the key design components that distinguish this approach from a more traditional approach to civic education. We conclude this section with a discussion of attempts to implement action civics on a larger scale.

Generation Citizen

The Generation Citizen curriculum starts with research and debate around student-generated issues that impact their lives (Generation Citizen, n.d.d). After reaching consensus on an issue, students then engage in further research through a root cause analysis. During this phase, students also begin drafting an initial action plan to address the issue. Once the class finalizes an action plan, they advocate for their ideas through petitions, commentaries, social media campaigns, and meetings with local government representatives. Educators are then encouraged to have their students formally present their action plans to community leaders through a Civics Day organized by Generation Citizen (n.d.b) staff. The program concludes with class reflections and having students "explore concrete ways to remain active, politically engaged citizens" (Generation Citizen, 2018).

Mikva Challenge

The Mikva Challenge (mikvachallenge.org) curricula offer several flexible programs, such as Project Soapbox (https://mikvachallenge.org/our-work/programs/project-soapbox), which helps students hone their public speaking skills around an idea they are passionate about; Student Voice Committee (https://teach.mikvachallenge.org/curriculum/student-voice-committee), which helps schools develop an after-school youth governance program; Elections in Action (https://mikvachallenge.org/blog/what-does-it-mean-to-be-an-elections-in-action-youth-leader), which focuses on campaigning and electoral politics; and News. Voice. Power. (http://mikvachallenge.org/wp-content/uploads/2014/10/NVP-final.pdf), which is a powerful news media literacy program.

The core program, however, is Issues to Action (https://mikvachallenge.org/our-work/programs/action-civics-classrooms/issues-to-action), a six-step youth activism curriculum. Throughout this action civics program, students "examine their communities, identify issues of importance to them, conduct intensive primary research about these issues, analyze power, develop strategies, and take action to impact policy—while reflecting on the process throughout" (Mikva Challenge, n.d.a).

Project Citizen

Project Citizen (www.civiced.org/project-citizen), a curriculum developed by the Center for Civic Education, is a program that focuses on monitoring and influencing public policy at the local and state levels. In this program, students collectively identify a problem in their community and conduct preliminary research. They then evaluate various solutions to the problem and develop their own public policy solution to the issue. The class then collaboratively develops an action plan and advocates for their proposed policy to local authorities. The culminating event of this program is a "public hearing showcase before a panel of civic-minded community members" (Center for Civic Education, n.d.d). Students then have the opportunity to compete against other classes in a state and national Project Citizen Showcase.

As noted by Project Citizen trainer Michael Trofi:

> The value of Project Citizen is that students learn the actual processes to become an engaged citizen. They are able to take a closer look not just at public policy, but also the process of how to actually enact change. It is important for students to research alternatives as well as focus on who you need to influence to enact change. The best Project Citizen experiences also bring in outside experts, particularly members of legislative bodies at the state, local, or even national level. (M. Trofi, personal communication, August 13, 2021)

Earth Force

Earth Force (earthforce.org) is more of an issue-oriented approach to action civics. Using its community action and problem-solving process, the goal is to create learning experiences at the intersection of civic engagement, environmental issues, and STEM education (Earth Force, n.d.). Similar to the other approaches, classes collectively research issues that affect their communities, although this program is specific to environmental challenges. The program's six steps include: (1) conducting a community environmental inventory, (2) selecting an issue, (3) researching policy and community practice, (4) choosing a goal and strategy, (5) planning and taking civic action, and (6) assessing student success (Earth Force, 2013).

Core Components of Quality Action Civics

Whether it is part of a specific curriculum or program, or more of a do-it-yourself version that you develop independently, there are seven core components of conducting quality action civics.

1. **Research and examine local community issues:** Action civics typically begins with student research and examination of their local community to identify key issues and challenges that they face.

2. **Select and refine the topic or issue, and conduct deeper levels of research:** Following deliberation, the class chooses a topic or issue and then engages in a deeper level or research, sometimes using a root-cause analysis or related process.

3. **Design public policy solutions:** Next, students design possible public policy solutions for the issue. One common mistake students make in this step is designing solutions that may be better suited for civil society or the business community. It is often helpful for educators to teach a specific lesson on what public policy actually entails and what types of issues and solutions fall within this sphere.

4. **Build consensus around a proposed solution:** Although it's tempting to have students work individually or in small groups, deliberation and consensus building are core features of action civics. Encourage large-group, or even whole-class projects. Teachers can use several different strategies to help narrow down the class topic, including categorizing ideas by theme instead of just ranking by the best choice. For example, students can categorize the topics by most practical, most impactful, or most creative.

5. **Reach out to community partners and government representatives:** While coming to consensus on proposed solutions, students might reach out to community partners, organizations, and government representatives to learn more in depth about the issue, their proposed actions, and what support they can garner.

6. **Engage in civic action to promote the chosen public policy proposal:** Once students develop a strategy, they engage in some type of civic action. This can come in many forms, but all involve some type of authentic experience with an audience beyond their peers and teacher. This could include presenting a proposal at a town council meeting, creating an online awareness campaign, or meeting with community leaders to propose a solution.

7. **Reflect on the civic action experience:** Action civics projects almost always conclude with some type of reflection on what new civic knowledge, skills, and dispositions students developed throughout the process.

Involving students in the core components of action civics provides them with a richer, more comprehensive experience and a deeper understanding of civic education. In our ever-changing world, there are many other elements you can weave into your instruction on action civics, including a variety of powerful technologies and digital resources.

Technologies to Enhance Action Civics

When thoughtfully applied, educators can use technologies to amplify the impact of great teaching and learning. This is no different when it comes to action civics. We are also witnessing firsthand how modern technologies are helping young people engage in activism across the world in new and engaging ways (van der Voo, 2020). It is therefore essential that educators weave many of these emerging digital tools into instructional practice and student projects. In the following sections, we highlight key technologies that educators can leverage during different phases of action civics projects.

Online Research

The following resources can help students in the initial research phase of their action civics projects.

- **AllSides (http://AllSides.com):** This website curates current events from over eight hundred media outlets and categorizes them by their ideological leanings. Early phases of action civics projects typically involve a substantial amount of student research, many times around topics that are political in nature. AllSides can help students identify different takes on a story based on their ideological leanings to help inform them of possible biases that could impact some of their research.
- **FactCheck.org:** This nonprofit, nonpartisan organization from the Annenberg Public Policy Center of the University of Pennsylvania fact-checks elected officials' claims. In the research phases of action civics, students can use FactCheck.org to help distinguish the credibility of claims for various viewpoints on issues they are investigating.

Collaboration, Deliberation, and Community Outreach

Many technologies can help foster dialogue and deliberation in both live and asynchronous ways that were previously impossible in classroom settings due to time and place constraints. No more! Check out these powerful tools to take classroom discussion and outreach to another level.

- **Flipgrid (info.flipgrid.com):** A rising star in the education technology world, Flipgrid is used by educators and students worldwide to engage in asynchronous video discussions. Teachers can leverage this tool for class discussions, particularly in the early phases of action research, which include a substantial amount of deliberations. Students also can use it as a tool to reach out to community members and elected officials to solicit information and feedback on action civics projects.

- **Google Meet (https://meet.google.com):** Meet is Google's live video conferencing tool that is free for all Google for Education school districts. This tool enables students to engage in live meetings with multiple students or community stakeholders virtually.

- **Zoom (https://zoom.us):** Like Google Meet, Zoom is a live videoconferencing tool with many advanced features for breakout rooms and other ways to manage the virtual experiences. Advanced features in Zoom, such as breakout rooms and live polling, can help make live meeting scenarios more engaging and effective to gauge audience thoughts and feedback.

Communication Tools for Advocacy

A key component of action civics is advocating for proposed change. Many technologies are designed specifically to help spread messages throughout a wider community. Following are several student-friendly options organized by types of media.

- **Images:** Canva (www.canva.com), Adobe Spark (www.adobe.com/express), Google Drawings (docs.google.com/drawings), Unsplash (https://unsplash.com), Pixabay (https://pixabay.com)

- **Videos:** iMovie (www.apple.com/imovie), Adobe Spark (adobe.com/express), WeVideo (www.wevideo.com)

- **Podcasts:** Anchor (https://anchor.fm), Synth (https://gosynth.com), Audacity (www.audacityteam.org), GarageBand (www.apple.com/mac/garageband)

- **Websites:** Google Sites (sites.google.com), Adobe Spark (www.adobe.com/express)

- **Social media campaigns:** Facebook (www.facebook.com), Instagram (instagram.com), Twitter (https://twitter.com), TikTok (www.tiktok.com)

Action Civics in Action

So, what does action civics actually look like *in action*? In this section, we explore student projects from various action civics programs representing students from diverse demographics and geographic locations.

Generation Citizen Projects

As discussed previously, Generation Citizen engages students in impactful learning experiences that transcend traditional civics curricula and can lead to meaningful action and change in students' local communities. For example, Willard Middle Schools' eighth-grade class sought to address the homelessness crisis in its community of Berkeley, California, by advocating for funding of a youth shelter (Generation Citizen, n.d.c). The students reached out to city officials and advocated to pass a resolution funding youth homeless shelters. After several rounds of advocacy, a key city official visited the class to hear the students' proposal directly and engage in a conversation with them. He agreed with the students but informed them that he alone could not make the decision. Instead, they would need to persuade a majority of city council members. The proposal was eventually introduced to the full city council, as students published correspondence to all council members in support of the policy proposal (Generation Citizen, n.d.c).

In another powerful example, a class at Lowell High School in Massachusetts sought to address the gun violence issue by advocating for a local gun buyback program (Generation Citizen, n.d.e). Students conducted further research on the issue and also petitioned local leaders to pass a red flag bill, a type of legislation that "temporarily remove[s] firearms from those who may be a harm to themselves or others" (Vasilogambros, 2021). Reflecting on the experience, one of the students, a refugee from Iraq, proclaimed that:

> When I have an idea or care deeply about an issue, I can speak up. . . . We . . . have the opportunity and responsibility to act—to speak up about the issues that affect our communities, to raise our voice, to become leaders. . . . I am only a student, but if I see an issue that needs fixing, I can work on it, indeed it is my responsibility to help fix it. (Generation Citizen, n.d.e)

The following interview with Jeff Grifka, social studies department chair at Kickemuit Middle School in Rhode Island and advocate for action civics programs, provides insight regarding how action civics programs can get up and running in K–12 schools.

Generation Citizen: Story From the Field

Q: Why did you decide to adopt the Generation Citizen action civics curriculum?

A: We saw significant gaps in civic education at the middle school level. What we did [was] seek out a program that would not only teach civic education, but have students get more engaged in it. Generation Citizen [helps students] get a background of civics, apply what they have learned by investigating issues in the community, and put ideas together to address it and enact change.

Q: What impact have you seen as a result of the past two years of action civics implementation?

A: The kids have done fantastic work. The voting group with the least turnout is [people] 18–25 [years old], since many don't feel like they can make a difference. This program helps them see that they can make change, as their voice is heard by the community. It is a powerful experience for kids to problem solve in a different way and even petition at the local and state levels. We had a number of state legislators come in to speak, hear from the students, and provide them with feedback. We also focus on the time and effort that they put into the project. The practice is valuable, and they have opportunities to investigate an issue. For instance, a student at the high school brought up the issue of having EpiPens on the bus. She pushed for state legislation, and it got traction and was eventually passed into law.

Q: Can you provide a few more examples of student projects?

A: Sure thing. One project focused on funding research for biodegradable fishing nets. One group led the charge for a local paper straw ban ordinance. Another group had a similar project that advocated for the removal of Styrofoam lunch trays and replacing them with paper trays.

Q: What are the major challenges of implementing action civics?

A: It is a shift for the teachers, since they are encouraged not to guide students in any particular direction regarding the public policy solution. You need to give students an opportunity to think outside the box and guide themselves. Also, student projects tend to be more liberal, but we should not limit students' opportunities to think freely.

Q: Any final thoughts to share?

A: Action civics gets students actively involved—what better way to learn it than getting involved in it? We need to learn by doing.

(J. Grifka, personal communication, January 23, 2020)

Constitutional Rights Foundation Civic Action Projects

You can find many examples of civic action projects (CAPs) curated by the Constitutional Rights Foundation. Despite the difference in terminology, CAPs and action civics projects are essentially the same thing. The Civic Action Project (2019) offers the following collection of civic action projects.

- A problem or issue that matters to students
- A public policy connection
- Discrete civic actions designed to engage civil society and other community stakeholders with their problem or issue
- The use of media to inform and engage their audience about their concern and suggested actions to support a solution

Topics include traffic safety, plastic bag bans, bus stops, public transportation, animal cruelty, and cyberbullying. Other examples focus on specific federal legislation such as the DREAM Act, which allows young people who arrived as undocumented children to apply for legal residency (Constitutional Rights Foundation, 2018).

One particularly impactful project called Inglewood Gentrification (Constitutional Rights Foundation, 2017) exemplifies how action civics programs engage students in the real work of active citizens. In this project, students began by researching gentrification and its effects on communities. They then began researching the new two-billion-dollar NFL stadium being built in Inglewood and studied its potential impacts on the surrounding areas. Their next step was to travel to neighborhoods in Inglewood to observe and engage in interviews with local residents. After conducting community polls, interviews, and outreach to local politicians, the students developed an online awareness campaign aimed at proposing rent control policies in Inglewood (Inglewood Gentrification Policy; https://iwgentrification2016.wixsite.com/savethecity). Their initial research on gentrification eventually led to civic action through public policy advocacy for rent control legislation.

Mikva Challenge Action Civics Projects

The Mikva Challenge Action Civics Showcase is an opportunity for students to share their projects with local community leaders. Visit the Mikva Challenge website (https://mikvachallenge.org) to see one of the showcases in action that highlights student projects focusing on various issues which are meaningful and impactful to their community, such as Youth Safety Advisory Council, Gay and Straight Alliance, Youth and Police Officer Relationships, Building Healthy Communities, and Combatting Mental Health Issues (Mikva Challenge, n.d.c).

Challenges of Action Civics

Despite the enthusiasm and momentum behind action civics programs, they are not without their challenges. First, some argue that action civics focuses too much on political issues and social justice while not enough on core understanding of the political system and underlying values. There is also the challenge that many students will gravitate toward ideas and issues that they already care deeply about and on which they have preconceived perspectives. Therefore, this process could further polarize their thinking along ideological lines. Some also contend that there is an underlying "progressive bias in the assumptions underlying many of the projects" (Kissel, 2019).

Adam Kissel (2019) published a list of action civics project ideas for conservative students to help balance out the conversation and provide educators with a broader spectrum of driving questions. Driving questions help guide student inquiry, typically during the brainstorming phase of public policy solutions. For example, how might we mitigate the unintended negative consequences of rent control in our community (Kissel, 2019)? Since action civics projects typically involve proposing an idea to a government authority, students may also be disillusioned if their proposal is not accepted and enacted (Wexler, 2020).

Another barrier is professional learning. Action civics is, in many ways, an inquiry- or project-based learning (PBL) pedagogy. Many educators may have heard of PBL, but the vast majority have not had any formal educator training in this instructional approach. Guidance and support for educators to plan and implement PBL are often necessary for action civics experiences to be as effective as possible. Conversely, students need to develop the skill sets and dispositions to thrive in a more student-centered, collaborative project setting.

Conclusion

It is no coincidence that the first topic we choose to focus on is action civics. All the shifts in approaches to civic education since the early 2000s focus on involving students in authentic experiences through which they actively engage in the work of citizens, which holds the greatest potential. Despite some claims to the contrary, you can apply action civics to a wide range of ideological viewpoints and provide students with real-world experiences in active citizenship and all its complexities. Due to these inherent complexities and challenges of advocating for ideas and developing consensus, the ability to engage in productive civil discourse is an essential corollary skill to civic action. We turn to this topic in the next chapter.

Key Takeaways for the Power of Action Civics and Authentic Experiences

Following are some key takeaways from this chapter on the power of action civics and authentic experiences.

- Action civics programs encourage students to identify and research societal issues, design public policy solutions to address them, and mobilize support for their public policy solutions. This approach aligns with research suggesting that authentic, project-based learning experiences lead to deeper student learning.

- Several action civics programs have emerged to help educators and students engage in this work with existing social studies courses and curricula. Two examples include Generation Citizen and the Mikva Challenge.

- Educational technology can play a key role in amplifying the impact of action civics in various phases of a student project, including research, collaboration, communication, and public mobilization.

Chapter 4

ENGAGEMENT IN CIVIL DISCOURSE

Imagine for a moment that you are riding in an elevator, and a stranger next to you shares a belief that is diametrically opposed to yours. The elevator is a unique environment in that nearly anything you do, other than face forward and track the passing floors, is frowned upon. Most people avoid interacting directly with others in the elevator and generally stay silent. We disengage. You might glance around to see how other riders are reacting, but you will likely stay quiet and hope one of you gets off the elevator quickly.

When it comes to politics, we are moving toward an elevator mentality. You could argue that the charged political environment in democracies around the world would seem to create a similar mentality not confined to a place, but instead connected to conversations about politics. A recent Pew Research Center report outlined some interesting trends (Jurkowitz & Mitchell, 2020).

- ▸ 45 percent of U.S. adults have stopped talking politics with someone because of their political beliefs.
- ▸ 58 percent of people who closely follow political news have stopped talking politics with someone because of their political beliefs.

- People who mostly follow local TV programming for political information are less likely to have stopped talking politics with someone because of their political beliefs.

- 50 percent of White adults, 37 percent of Black adults, and 34 percent of Hispanic adults have stopped talking politics with someone because of their political beliefs.

- 47 percent of women and 43 percent of men have stopped talking politics with someone because of their political beliefs.

Democracy as an institution is built on a foundation of civil discourse in which citizens work to resolve their differences peacefully through a democratic process. What this evidence demonstrates is that healthy political discourse is in decline. It is a trend that needs to be reversed so we don't end up stuck silently in a political elevator.

Civil discourse can be described as "robust, honest, frank, and constructive dialogue and deliberation that seek to advance the public interest" (Leskes, 2013). Civil discourse can be hard to come by in today's classrooms. Classroom teachers who choose to take on controversial issues risk being accused of bias and partiality from one side of the political spectrum or another. For classroom teachers, the temptation is to take the safe path and stick to teaching textbook facts about the government and the Constitution. The current political climate makes it more likely that curricula addressing these topics will be cast in a negative light or labeled partisan (Jamieson, 2013). This strategy has a harmful effect on students' future understanding of and participation in democracy.

Students from socioeconomically disadvantaged households have fewer opportunities to learn about and engage in democratic processes than those with a higher socioeconomic status. The lack of opportunities has an adverse effect on their future behavior (Atwell et al., 2017). Often, poorer students live in civic deserts. These are areas "without adequate opportunities for civic engagement—places for discussing issues, addressing problems together, forming relationships of mutual support" (Atwell et al., 2017, p. 5). Sixty percent of rural students and approximately one-third of urban and suburban students perceive themselves to live in a civic desert (Atwell et al., 2017).

At the same time, you should not assume that just because students are from a wealthier community, they will automatically engage in democratic processes. It's more likely to occur, but even wealthier students live in a civic desert if they don't have a chance to connect with the opportunities around them. This civics gap is perpetuated by schools if they do not create meaningful civil discourse experiences for students.

In this chapter, you will learn about the meaning of civil discourse, why some teachers might avoid it in their classrooms, and strategies for teaching democratic values through civil discourse.

Why Many Teachers Don't Engage in Civil Discourse With Students

To fulfill their important role in society, schools and teachers need to run *to*—not *from*—the challenges presented by the divisive political climate that exists in democracies across the world. The role of schools as a key player in the success of U.S. democracy is older than the Constitution itself, which was created in September of 1787. Under the Articles of Confederation, the Land Ordinance of 1785 set aside land from each new township for the support of schools. This was followed by the Northwest Ordinance in July 1787, which declared that schools and education shall forever be encouraged. Schools were key to the plans of the founding fathers to preserve democracy by preparing citizens to understand and participate in it (Jamieson, 2013).

Ronald Reagan referred to this legacy in a radio address in 1988, saying "Since the founding of this nation, education and democracy have gone hand in hand" (Reagan, 1988). It is for these reasons that when the Carnegie Corporation of New York and CIRCLE (2003) published their report on the state of civic education in 2003, they named it *Guardian of Democracy* (Gould et al., 2011). What's more, Americans have come to expect that schools will prepare citizens, nurture their civic pride, and instill them with common values. Those seeking educational reform have noted that civic education is not as tied to public schools as it has been in the past.

One reason that teachers have stepped back from this role of preparing citizens to understand and participate in a democracy is disagreement over how to define the role of the citizen in a democracy. Are we trying to replicate and sustain democracy as is, or are we looking to create citizens to reconstruct democratic society in the name of, for example, justice and inclusivity? This disagreement might be a good place to start a civil discourse among students and is an example of how a simple textbook understanding of democracy does little to teach them about perhaps the most important aspects of democratic society: how we resolve our differences peacefully and respectfully, as well as the consequences when we fail to do so.

How to Teach Democratic Values Through Civil Discourse

So, what types of experiences should we include in civic education to make sure that students understand democratic values? We can begin by teaching less about citizenship and providing students with more actual experience being citizens. The following activities can help students experience what it means to be a democratic citizen.

- Participate in local government.
- Address relevant, real-life problems.
- Debate different topics.
- Create class norms.
- Participate in class dialogues.
- Engage in virtual discourse.
- Complete civic action projects.
- Explore controversial topics.

Participate in Local Government

An obvious place to start is to provide opportunities for students to reach out and participate in local government. In the past, this might have meant taking students to watch a government proceeding such as a town council or school board meeting. But why not offer students the chance to do more than watch passively? Why not have them take part by developing and sharing a position? This might also take the form of proposing a program or course of action.

In 2015, a group of New Hampshire fourth graders proposed a law that would name the red-tailed hawk as the state bird. The class had constructed the law as part of a unit on how a bill becomes a law. The hawk was their school mascot. The students followed the law as it proceeded past a close vote in the Agriculture Committee, where it passed by a 10–8 vote (Claffey, 2015).

On the day that the bill was finally to get its vote by the full New Hampshire House, the students were excited and hopeful. But once floor debate began, several representatives took the floor to oppose the law. One lawmaker called the bill ridiculous and suggested that if they passed the bill naming a state bird, they would soon find themselves naming an official state hot dog. Another state lawmaker declared that the red-tailed hawk might make a better mascot for Planned Parenthood (Claffey, 2015). When the dust settled and the votes were counted, the measure failed to pass by a margin of 133–160, while the class sat and watched from the gallery.

The story got national news coverage and was even the subject of a segment on *Last Week Tonight With John Oliver* (Oliver, 2015). Many of the news stories suggested that this was a missed opportunity to teach the students an important lesson about government. The students were interviewed and shared their frustration that their bill was not taken seriously and struggled to understand the viewpoints of the legislators who had voted against it. One student shared that they didn't want to become a representative because they felt that representatives were mean. Fortunately, the story didn't end there (Biello & Cohen, 2019).

In 2019, those same students, now eighth graders, brought the bill back to the New Hampshire House to try again. The original sponsor of the bill felt that it was important to give the bill that mattered so much to these students a second chance (Biello & Cohen, 2019). This time, lawmakers knew that the bill had broad public support, and after four years, the students were able to watch their idea become a law, passing by a vote of 333–11 (Ramer, 2019).

While the path may have been bumpy, the experience was probably more meaningful because it *didn't* go as planned. Instead, students learned about the power of public opinion, the role of the media, and how to overcome their initial loss. Compare this experience to what students would have learned if the teacher had simply shared a lecture about how a bill becomes a law.

Address Relevant, Real-Life Problems

The lesson of the red-tailed hawk is interesting because it didn't need to become controversial. As John Oliver said in his rebuke of the New Hampshire House of Representatives, "This doesn't matter; just vote yes and make them happy!" (Oliver, 2015). To some advocates of teaching citizenship, this is exactly the problem. They believe that we should be engaging students in taking on the real problems that they face in the community. The *lived civics* approach emphasizes theories and practices rooted in and responsive to the lived reality of young people with a focus on race and ethnicity. In *Let's Go There: Making a Case for Race, Ethnicity and a Lived Civics Approach to Civic Education*, Cohen and colleagues (2018) state:

> Viewing education through the lens of race, ethnicity, and other identities changes how civics curriculum is taught and how youth civic engagement programming is developed. It also changes students' experiences in the classroom. When educators attend to the lived experiences of students, particularly young people of color, classrooms become places where young people's expertise becomes central to addressing the challenges of democracy. (pp. 4–5)

Focusing on the lived experiences of students of color has a powerful impact on their civic identities. Doing so is more meaningful than addressing the typical scenarios presented in a textbook that rarely address experiences that are relevant to their lives. Students of color feel a disconnect between the values they are taught in government classes and the social and political truths they see firsthand (Rubin & Hayes, 2010). Textbooks don't regularly include examples that align with their view of the world.

Debate Different Topics

One of the most common practices used to develop skills necessary for civil discourse is debate. Classroom debates not only help students formulate an opinion and defend it, but also listen to others and engage in conversation. Classroom debates provide opportunities to teach argumentation, and students who understand how arguments are constructed are better able to analyze others' arguments and evaluate their effectiveness.

Research on the benefits of debate is clear. Students across grade levels who participate in classroom debates and debate activities are more engaged and motivated. Debate encourages them to apply their learning and fosters critical-thinking skills. Students benefit from socially constructed learning (Ackerman, Neale, & CfBT Education Trust, 2011).

Engaging in debate allows students to use information to construct arguments and evaluate the strength of those arguments. It doesn't hurt for them to also evaluate weaker arguments or the use of misleading or false statements, such as logical fallacies. Understanding logical fallacies is an important citizenship skill. A *logical fallacy* is "a false statement that weakens an argument by distorting an issue, drawing false conclusions, misusing evidence, or misusing language" (Kemper, Meyer, Van Rys, & Sebranek, 2018, p. 261). While teaching about logical fallacies might be a good start, having students identify and construct logical fallacies better prepares them to identify fallacies in the real world.

Following are some examples of common logical fallacies (Lumen Learning, n.d.). Why not make responding to logical fallacies part of the debate experience?

▸ **Ad hominem:** In this fallacy, a person comments on someone's character rather than the argument. For example, during a debate or discussion, a person verbally attacks their opponent's personal characteristics rather than focusing on the topic of the debate.

▸ **Appeal to ignorance:** In this fallacy, a person influences someone to agree with their beliefs, even with no supporting evidence. For example, a person's blanket-statement opinion about people in another political party leads to stereotypes that others believe.

- **Red herring:** In this fallacy, a person aims to divert someone away from the main issue of discussion. For example, a concerned teacher asks a student about a low exam grade, and the student brings up another issue to steer the teacher away from the uncomfortable topic.
- **Straw man:** In this fallacy, a person misrepresents the view or idea of their opponent in order to persuade someone to agree with their viewpoint. For example, politicians might make ludicrous claims to undermine their opponent's viewpoint, making their own viewpoint more appealing.

Create Class Norms

A best practice for conducting discussions and debate is for teachers to create class guidelines, a class contract, or clear norms about expectations during debates. Facing History and Ourselves (2016) suggests that teachers should guide their classes in creating their own set of norms, rather than providing one. The teacher can then post the class norms so they serve as a reminder of the agreement students made and can be referenced as needed. During a heated discussion, a teacher might say, "Thank you for sharing your thoughts on that topic. I want to pause here and remind everyone to refer to our class norms. We all agreed that we would focus criticism on ideas and not on individuals. Can I ask you to rephrase that last comment in a way that reflects that norm?"

While there are powerful examples of classroom norms for discussing controversial topics available online, one valuable strategy is to actively construct class norms for these discussions with your students. The process can begin with some simple, honest questions.

- "What makes discussing controversial topics hard?"
- "What do you worry about when discussing topics on which we disagree?"

The teacher can then construct a discussion around these worries and fears to create class understandings about how to navigate such debates. Similar student suggestions can be distilled into common language, and the discussion of key concerns will help the class understand the needs of other classmates.

While doing this with a class of freshmen, one problem kept repeating itself: classroom discussions are always dominated by a few louder, more extroverted students who may not be the most knowledgeable source on any given topic. This makes it hard for more introverted students to find a place to share. Working together as a class, we discussed ways to include more voices in discussions. To our surprise, what we created was an effective strategy to foster participation. All classroom discussions took place by bringing three desks to the center of the room. One of those desks was labeled *First-Time Speakers Only*. This meant that there would always be a place open for any person who had not spoken to the class yet. Speaking took place in the order in which students came forward, which removed the anxiety of waiting to be called on.

Over time, we developed other rules, such as labeling one of the desks *I Have Spoken More Than Three Times*. As a result, these guidelines regulated discussion, which changed the teacher role, allowing more focus on the ideas being shared rather than moderating participation. More voices were elevated, and a healthier conversation took place.

There are many frameworks and guidelines for creating classroom norms, such as keeping the list short and keeping positive framing such as, "We value _____, so we will _____." What all the guidelines have in common is this: students are more likely to embrace a set of principles they have a hand in creating. This strategy also has the added benefit of modeling democratic principles.

Participate in Class Dialogues

Debate may not always be the most effective way to generate civil discourse. In fact, using debate too often might give students the impression that every sharing of different opinions should be a debate. Debates have at their core a desire to win by changing people's minds. Debates put students in a position of listening not to understand but to counter what their opponent says. The distinction between a debate and a dialogue can be unclear, but it is important to model for students that one can present ideas without the intention of swaying people but rather with the goal of broadening the perspectives of participants. Often when we say that we want to encourage debate, what we really want to encourage is a healthy dialogue.

Table 4.1 lists some of the distinct differences among discussion, debate, and dialogue.

Table 4.1: Differences Among Discussion, Debate, and Dialogue

Discussion	Debate	Dialogue
Offers thoughts and ideas	Achieves or wins	Broadens personal perspective
Seeks answers and solutions	Seeks weaknesses	Seeks shared meaning
Persuades others	Emphasizes disagreements	Identifies areas of agreement
Shares information	Focuses on right or wrong	Uncovers areas of ambivalence
Avoids conflict and differences	Emphasizes conflict and differences	Articulates conflict and differences
Maintains relationships	Ignores relationships	Builds relationships

Source: Adapted from Kachwaha, 2002.

Engage in Virtual Discourse

Regardless of what we may see as negative effects of online conversations, it's clear that people are engaging with each other online as part of the international discussion of politics. It is also likely that students engage in online conversations using social media. One reason that social media has become a place to tread lightly is the prevalence of online incivility, especially in places where anonymity exists. Beyond teaching students about proper online behavior, we can help them identify the kinds of places where incivility is likely to exist.

People are more likely to remain respectful in places where their identities are known. This is important for teachers to keep in mind in making sure that they are choosing the right places for their students to participate in online discourse. Online conversations can go bad, and online bullying is a real concern. Therefore, many online news sites have stopped allowing comments on their stories. Teachers can address that issue by creating experiences for students that allow them to learn prosocial online norms and behaviors. Common Sense Media (n.d.) offers the following advice about what to teach children about safe online behavior.

- **Communicate appropriately:** Know your audience and choose your language accordingly.
- **Keep private information private:** Know what *not* to share. What you post online can live there for a long time. Your personal information, address, phone number, gossip, and photos can have consequences now and in the future.

- **Be respectful:** Treat others with dignity. When you disagree online, there is a right way and a wrong way. How you treat others is visible to the world and searchable to others.

- **Don't lie, steal, or cheat:** Speak truthfully. Act honestly. Always give attributions when sharing the work of others. If you would like to borrow something, ask first. The answer to the question, "Who will know if I take this?" is "Everyone."

- **Act as an upstander:** If you see someone treating another in a cruel or unkind way, stand up for them.

- **Report inappropriate behavior:** Use reporting tools to notify online platforms of the mistreatment. If enough people call out a behavior, it can be addressed.

- **Respect the rules set by your family:** Follow family rules such as *no phones in your bedroom* and *no texting at the table*. Ask before you download that new app. Parents have expectations for your behavior in person or online. If you aren't sure how to apply their rules to a new online situation, ask.

- **Pause and consider the consequences before you post anything:** Deleting something once you have had second thoughts may not be enough to undo the damage caused by a misunderstood or mistyped comment. The consequences can be high and long lasting. The internet will remember the error long after the mistake is made, and what you say may not be as well received outside your immediate circle of friends.

Class blogs and school-run discussion rooms provide students with experiences you can use as a foundation for the skills they will need online later in life. The following list provides some examples of digital resources you can use to create opportunities for dialogue.

- **Flipgrid (info.flipgrid.com):** Students can respond to prompts shared by the teacher and then view the responses left by others. The platform allows for teacher moderation so responses can be reviewed before becoming public. Because students are recording their responses, they can be more thoughtful about what they say and can re-record their responses if needed. This tool has the advantage of allowing students who are more introverted to participate in ways with which they might not feel comfortable if the discussions took place in person.

- **Padlet (https://padlet.com):** Padlet allows for students to post responses in the form of text images or audio files. As a tool for civil discourse, it allows people to share their thoughts for review by others.
- **Class blogs:** An important citizenship skill is formulating and sharing opinions. Blogs are exceptional for this purpose. You can keep blogs private or shared, and allow students to engage in smaller-scale dialogues that help them build the skills and attitudes of civil discourse.
- **Wonder (https://wonder.me) and Gather (www.gather.town):** Both tools allow students to create virtual gathering places where they can participate in discussions. Students can move between a variety of conversations as they navigate through a virtual gathering. You can use both tools to create smaller dialogues to build skills before asking students to participate in larger-scale dialogues.
- **Google Docs or Microsoft Word:** In the absence of other platforms, you can use these tools to create shared documents for peer editing and leaving comments for classmates. While in a basic form, you can change up these activities from basic commentary, to leaving feedback on blogs, and participating on more common social platforms.

Having students use social media in lessons may not always be possible, but you can model good behavior and teach skills by creating classroom social media accounts through which they can engage online collectively under teacher supervision. This is an area where running *to*—rather than *from*—the problem is a good practice.

Class Twitter accounts are common among teachers to reach out to public figures and share what the class is working on. You might allow students to craft messages for sharing. If they are prepared to do so, social media can do a lot to educate and connect students and serve as a tool to engage with local officials and elected leaders. We need students to commit to the belief that a democracy does not mean we won't have disagreements, but it allows us to resolve our differences respectfully and peacefully.

Complete Civic Action Projects

Civic action projects are built around the following four characteristics (Civic Action Project, 2019a).

1. A problem or issue that matters to students
2. A public policy connection
3. Discrete civic actions designed to engage civil society and other community stakeholders with their problem or issue

4. The use of media to inform and engage their audience about their concern and suggested actions to support a solution

These student projects reflect the values of the students and focus on environmental concerns, public safety, mental health, social justice, and just about anything else that students identify as an issue in their daily lives. These include the following:

- Bullying and violence on campus
- School safety
- School food waste
- Gender equality in the workplace
- Homelessness and affordable housing
- Public transportation
- The minimum wage
- Animal cruelty
- Gun control
- Underage drinking
- Immigration

For example, the Boys and Girls Clubs of Central Florida After School Zone at Wolf Lake Middle School was enthusiastic about partnering with Orange County Public Schools (OCPS) to explore an interrogation of expansive safety measures under current policy. As a result of this partnership, the OCPS considered the following safety measures: installing panic buttons in each classroom for teachers, requiring everyone on campus to wear identification badges, and establishing classroom security checks (Civic Action Project, 2019b).

Not every student project results in a change in government policy, but some do. In the process, students learn about what it takes to set a policy goal, inform the public, and move the wheels of government. Students who participate in experiences like these are far more likely to exhibit civic self-efficacy and civic knowledge and are more likely to connect to others who are knowledgeable about civic and political life (Ballard, Cohen, & Littenberg-Tobias, 2016).

Explore Controversial Topics

Teachers can improve their class's ability to discuss challenging or controversial topics by creating a classroom culture that is ready to handle them. Setting clear classroom norms, creating the right environment—either virtually or in person—and preparing students and their parents for discussing controversial topics put teachers in the position to not only plan to address challenging topics head on, but also to be prepared for them when they arise unexpectedly. When a challenging conversation suddenly appears, avoiding it is the worst thing a teacher can do. It shows the class that avoiding the conversation is a valid strategy. If we want students to become effective democratic citizens, we must prepare them with the skills and attitudes to engage with each other when those situations arise.

Facing History and Ourselves (n.d.a) offers the following tips for discussing controversial issues.

- Listen to understand before you react and form an opinion. Use *I* statements.

- When you don't feel safe commenting on or questioning openly in class, be sure to document your thoughts anyway. Ask for teacher support in finding the safest way to share your idea with the class. (Online class discussion can provide students a sense of safety they won't have in person.)

- Identify others who contribute thoughts or ideas that help you grow. Let them know that you benefited from their contributions.

- If you find another person's contributions hurtful or offensive, respond to the hurt that the comment, and not the person, caused. Include why the comment caused you to feel that way. Others in the class may gain understanding from your explanation. It's never okay to attack or belittle others.

- It's important to ask about what you do not understand.

- Let your thoughts and not your emotions guide your thinking.

- Make sure that everyone has the opportunity to contribute to the discussion.

- Respect those who are speaking by allowing them to complete their comments before you respond.

- Not every idea is going to be shared. Document those that you don't get to share. Write thoughts in your journal if you don't have time to say them during class.

- Journaling during a discussion can be powerful, but you need not share every idea that you document.

Discussing controversial topics can be challenging, but learning how to do it effectively prepares students to deal with these situations both inside and outside of school. It's a skill they will use throughout their lifetimes.

Conclusion

We need to ensure that students have rich opportunities to engage in civil discourse—like the activities outlined in this chapter—no matter where they live or what their socioeconomic background. Exploring controversial topics allows students to develop their own unique voice and the ability to share their beliefs and values effectively. These discussions are valuable, even if they don't change anyone's mind, simply because they teach students how to process opposing views and have a deeper understanding of issues.

Students can't learn the behavioral norms for discussing highly charged or political topics if they are never placed in a situation where they do so. Creating the right environment and building a strong classroom culture for these conversations to take place require time and energy, but the investment is worth the effort, since democracy as an institution rests on the foundation that civil discourse creates.

Key Takeaways for Engagement in Civil Discourse

Following are key takeaways from this chapter on engagement in civil discourse.

- ▸ Civil discourse is key to understanding how a democracy works and demonstrates how we can resolve our differences peacefully and respectfully.
- ▸ Differences in how we define the role of a citizen can cause conflict. Having conversations on the topic is a good way to foster understanding and clarify exactly what we are asking teachers to do.
- ▸ Having students participate in local government teaches students in a way that reflects their lived reality, is relevant to their lives, and powerfully impacts their civic identities.
- ▸ Allowing students to create class norms surrounding debates can help teachers build a class culture suited to challenging conversations.
- ▸ Debate may not always be the best environment to gain understanding. Dialogue focuses less on proving a point in order to pursue broadening perspectives and more fully understanding the issues.

- Virtual discourse can offer many benefits in addition to teaching norms for online behavior. Many tools can serve as a platform for discourse that can also bring students into conversations that they might not participate in face to face.
- Civic action projects allow students to learn about issues and engage in the mechanisms of democracy to move the wheels of government, making them more likely to continue to do so later in life.
- Tackling controversial issues in class provides a platform for teaching students healthy norms and the skills necessary to engage with others when they disagree.

Chapter 5

NEWS MEDIA LITERACY FOR COMBATING MISINFORMATION

What is *misinformation*, and how is that different from *disinformation*? In what ways do news and social media amplify the spread of misinformation? What roles do schools play in addressing these challenges? What are the best civic education resources and strategies to help students navigate this complex and evolving element of citizenship? These are the driving questions that will guide you through this chapter.

Let's start with *misinformation*. Abrams (2021) refers to *misinformation* as "any claims or depictions that are inaccurate," while *disinformation* is "a subset of misinformation intended to mislead." Although we primarily use the term *misinformation* throughout this chapter, many of the examples could fall under that subset of *disinformation*. The problem, however, is not just that misinformation is out there—it is also that an alarming percentage of people is believing and sharing it with others. Although there are many reasons why people are susceptible to misinformation, evidence points to a set of key drivers. First, recent studies assert that "people deploy skepticism selectively—for instance, when they're less critical of ideas that align with their political beliefs" (Abrams, 2021). In other words, if the misinformation aligns with their current belief systems, they are more likely to accept the information as truth without hesitation. Individual differences can also play a role, as "people who use an intuitive reasoning style tend to believe fake news more often than those who rely primarily on analytical reasoning" (Abrams, 2021). A third key factor is based on political ideology. Research suggests that "those holding extreme beliefs . . . [are] most susceptible to misinformation" (Abrams, 2021).

So how do people find, access, and share misinformation? This is where the news media and social media come into play, a topic which we explore in great depth throughout the chapter. One common trend, whether it is from an established news outlet or a social media feed, is that news consumers must grapple with small snippets of information that often provide little background context regarding the issue or event. It is also increasingly difficult for people to discern between factual statements, opinions, or those that lie in a murky middle ground.

A Pew Research Center study found that "the basic task of differentiating between factual and opinion news statements presents somewhat of a challenge" (Desilver, 2018). In hindsight, since this survey was conducted, we attest that this study's assertion was a massive understatement. A more recent 2021 Pew Research Center study claims that "the climate in some segments of social media and other online spaces has been called a 'dumpster fire' of venom, misinformation, conspiracy theories, and goads to violence" (Anderson & Rainie, 2021). "Controlling the Spread of Misinformation" came to the conclusion that "passive sharers, rather than malicious actors, may be the bigger problem in the fake news phenomenon" (Abrams, 2021). We therefore cannot solely blame a small subset of society that creates this damaging content. The fires of misinformation are stoked by many everyday citizens who are passively sharing the content across their networks and social circles. The dangers of misinformation are real, which brings us to the aftermath of the 2020 presidential election.

Of all the obstacles facing teachers during the pandemic-dominated 2020–2021 school year, January 7, 2021, posed another significant challenge. The day after the protests at the U.S. Capitol—what some described as an insurrection and attack on democratic institutions—teachers and school leaders were unsure of how to address this topic with their classes. Educational organizations across the United States rapidly developed teaching materials, and school districts scrambled to provide guidance to staff and messaging to families. For example, the New York City Department of Education (n.d.) created a website, including a letter from the chancellor, along with an exhaustive list of civics-related teaching resources.

Despite these efforts, it was abundantly clear that despite the need for schools to help students navigate these troubling and consequential events, most were unprepared for the task. What makes this all the more frustrating is that we cannot honestly claim that these events were unpredictable or that schools had no way to lay the foundation needed to adequately rise to the occasion.

One of the major contributing factors that led to the events of January 6, 2021, was the underlying falsehoods and conspiracy theories that guided the protestors' actions. In fact, an unmistakable undercurrent of the entire 2020 U.S. presidential election was the increasing role of misinformation and its viral spread across all communication channels. One of the clearest impacts that this has had is the increasing cynicism some people feel toward the media, and in some cases, any political information regardless of the platform.

In a Knight Foundation (2018) Gallup study, 59 percent of respondents thought that the news media "was responsible in its reporting of the election results and outcomes." When the data were disaggregated along party lines, the numbers were more dismal. Only 17 percent of Republicans polled "believed news media projections of Joe Biden as the winner of the election were accurate" (Jones, 2020).

In an election in which numerous investigations and court cases disputing the election results concluded that the election results were, in fact, accurate, how is this possible? More than fifty lawsuits alleging voter fraud were ultimately dismissed in state and federal courts, while U.S. election security officials asserted that the 2020 election was "the most secure in American history" (Reuters, 2021). What has led to a situation in which millions of Americans do not trust the validity of their own electoral process? Even more troubling, what role did this sentiment play in the January 6, 2021 protests around the U.S. Capitol?

In this chapter, you will learn more about the dangers of misinformation and how it can affect the perspectives and actions of democratic citizens. News and information literacy is more important than ever, and we discuss how teachers can educate students in how to disseminate and analyze the barrage of information coming at them every day.

The Dangers of Misinformation

One example of misinformation is the Pizzagate conspiracy, during which online message boards spread a false story about a pizza restaurant that allegedly was the home of a Democratic party–connected child-trafficking ring. This story ultimately led to violence. A man who believed in the conspiracy involving the child-abuse ring opened fire at the restaurant with an assault rifle, later claiming that he was attempting to rescue "children [who] were being harbored in the restaurant" (Kang & Goldman, 2016). Four years after the initial Pizzagate hoax, the conspiracy theory returned, fueled by a comment on Justin Bieber's Instagram feed, which quickly spread on other platforms like TikTok (#PizzaGate hashtag viewed over 82 million times) and QAnon message boards (Kang & Frenkel, 2020).

A second example of how misinformation can lead to real harm is the proliferation of false information and conspiracy theories around COVID-19. Early on in the pandemic, the World Health Organization (WHO), the United Nations (UN), the International Conservation and Education Fund (INCEF), and other worldwide organizations released a joint statement to combat "deliberate attempts to disseminate wrong information to undermine the public health response." They went on to state that "mis- and disinformation can be harmful to people's physical and mental health; increase stigmatization; threaten precious health gains; and lead to poor observance of public health measures, thus reducing their effectiveness and endangering countries' ability to stop the pandemic" (World Health Organization, 2020).

"Controlling the Spread of Misinformation" directly tied the spread and consumption of COVID-19 misinformation to detrimental changes in behavior. According to the study, "hundreds of deaths and thousands of hospitalizations around the world [have been] associated with COVID-19 misinformation, including rumors, conspiracy theories, and stigmas" (Abrams, 2021).

But there is good news on this front. Educational research points to news media literacy as a core element of effective civic education (Levine & Kawashima-Ginsberg, 2017). There also has been a rapid proliferation of educational resources and online tools to help students develop these essential competencies. These resources and online tools are included throughout the rest of the chapter. We now turn to ways that schools and educators can help better prepare the next generation of citizens to access information, evaluate its validity, and engage in informed civil discourse.

News Media Literacy Education

Although Kavanagh and Rich's (2018) RAND report cites educational institutions as a contributing driver of what we refer to as *truth decay*, schools are also part of the solution. According to the report:

> Competing demands and fiscal constraints on the educational system have reduced the emphasis on civic education, media literacy, and critical thinking. Students need exactly this type of knowledge and these skills to effectively evaluate information sources, identify biases, and separate fact from opinion and falsehood. This gap between the challenges of the information system and the training provided to students drives and perpetuates Truth Decay by contributing to the creation of an electorate that is susceptible to consuming and disseminating disinformation, misinformation, and information that blur the line between fact and opinion.

Although this may seem like an indictment of schools, and in some ways it is, the takeaway here for us is that devoting more time and resources to civic education and the effective teaching of news media literacy can in fact help combat truth decay.

More specifically related to students, research suggests that their ability to decipher the validity of information online is no better than adults', and in some cases, worse. A sobering study from the Stanford History Education Group (SHEG; 2016) finds that students' skill set in this area is troubling:

> Our "digital natives" may be able to flit between Facebook and Twitter while simultaneously uploading a selfie to Instagram and texting a friend. But when it comes to evaluating information that flows through social media channels, they are easily duped. (p. 4)

In this study, which included thousands of students, 82 percent of middle school students mistook advertisements for news (SHEG, 2016). High school students did not fare much better, assuming that an image that was anonymously shared on a photo-sharing platform was proof of a nuclear disaster and its effects on the environment. Even college students left much to be desired. Many rated a group of pediatricians often labeled as a hate group as a more reputable source of information than the American Academy of Pediatrics (SHEG, 2016). As SHEG founder and Stanford professor Sam Wineburg (n.d.) puts it, "Our students are speeding along the information superhighway without a license. Before letting them loose, let's at least make sure they've passed the driving test."

When designing these experiences, schools can source from several U.S. organizations who provide the necessary research and guidance to follow. You may recall that news media literacy education is considered one of the complementary practices advocated in the foundational *The Republic Is (Still) at Risk—and Civics Is Part of the Solution* (Levine & Kawashima-Ginsberg, 2017) briefing, stating that this topic has "profound implications for youth participation" (p. 5). Several frameworks and definitions of these skills are provided by reputable groups such as Common Sense Media, News Literacy Project, SHEG, Media Literacy Now, and more.

Now, let's turn to specific tools and curricular resources that can help educators enhance news and information literacy in their classes.

News Media Literacy Activities

Educators can certainly benefit from the rapid development of news media literacy curricula, but the sheer volume of emerging resources can be overwhelming. We have, therefore, decided not to provide an exhaustive list of everything available, but instead highlight those that we deem the highest quality and classroom ready. In other words, the resource and curriculum programs in the pages that follow are well-researched and designed specifically for educators to use with their students. For each program, we also spotlight a specific activity and sample lesson that exemplify its approach and style.

Using Lateral Reading

The cornerstone strategy of this activity is *lateral reading*, which is "leaving a site to see what other digital sources say about it" (Civic Online Reasoning, n.d.e). The premise is that to learn about the validity of a site, you must leave it. Although this sounds counterintuitive, research demonstrates that seeing what other websites say about a source is often more illustrative of its validity than what a source says about itself (Civic Online Reasoning, n.d.e). The free curriculum includes over fifty lessons curated around the three following driving questions, including hands-on student activities and interactive media and video lessons (Civic Online Reasoning, n.d.a).

1. Who's behind the information?
2. What's the evidence?
3. What do other sources say?
   › **Organization:** Stanford History Education Group
   › **Grade range:** 6–12
   › **Key topics:** Evaluating claims on social media, determining website reliability, and identifying trustworthy evidence

Lesson spotlight: *Using lateral reading*—In "Lateral Reading vs. Vertical Reading" (Civic Online Reasoning, n.d.d), the teacher first demonstrates reading a website vertically, pointing out features such as URLs, content, and appearance. The teacher then models lateral reading strategies focused on learning about the source's "perspective, authority, and potential motivations for providing information" (Civic Online Reasoning, n.d.d). Students then engage in a case study employing both reading strategies and evaluate which led to a more accurate assessment of the source's validity (Civic Online Reasoning, n.d.d).

Understanding Bias

The News Literacy Project (NLP; n.d.a) is an educational nonprofit that offers several high-quality programs for educators that focus on helping students become "smart, active consumers of news and information and equal and engaged participants in a democracy." Their vast resource library has a curation of various lesson ideas, multimedia, and assessments related to teaching news literacy (News Literacy Project, n.d.d). Additionally, NLP developed Checkology, a free e-learning platform designed for students in grades 6–12 that includes interactive games and lessons around principles such as identifying credible information and seeking reliable sources (Checkology, n.d.b). For teachers in grades 4–6, the new "Is It 'Checkable'?" activity and resource guide are designed specifically for upper-elementary students (News Literacy Project, n.d.b).

Another high-quality resource aimed at helping educators is The Sift (News Literacy Project, n.d.e), a free weekly newsletter that highlights misinformation and related themes trending in the media. Each newsletter is accompanied by activities, discussion prompts, and links to resources to spark lively class discussions around the topics.

- **Organization:** News Literacy Project
- **Grade range:** 4–12
- **Key topics:** Identifying credible information, seeking reliable sources, applying critical-thinking skills to separate fact-based content from falsehoods

Lesson spotlight: *Understanding bias*—In this Checkology module, students take a deep dive into five different categories of media bias. Types of bias with embedded real-world scenarios include partisan, demographic, corporate, neutrality, and big story. Throughout the activity, students grapple with the complexity of bias, such as how one's ideas and worldview can influence their own perception of media bias (Checkology, n.d.a).

Exposing the Motives of Misinformation

Within a comprehensive and highly rated Digital Citizenship Curriculum (Common Sense Education, n.d.), Common Sense Media has created a core topic around news and media literacy. The instructional approach is unique in two ways. First, the focus beyond credible sources seeks to incorporate students' personal experiences in ways that keep them critically engaged in the process without becoming overly cynical (Common Sense Education, 2018). Second, *fairness* actively avoids "creating or implying a hierarchy of credible news sources" (Common Sense Education, 2018). Instead, it promotes students using their preferred media sources and platforms but doing so "more effectively and critically" (Common Sense Education, 2018). Each of the curriculum's thirteen lessons is designed in developmentally appropriate ways by grade level. For example, the kindergarten lesson's driving question involves finding a balance between online and offline activities, while the grade 12 lesson explores the complex nature of *filter bubbles*, which are "the results of the algorithms that dictate what we encounter online" (Farnam Street Media, n.d.). Filter bubbles alter the way we encounter ideas and information.

- **Organization:** Common Sense Media
- **Grade range:** K–12
- **Key topics:** Identifying credible and trustworthy information sources and reflecting on their responsibilities as thoughtful media creators and consumers

Lesson spotlight: *Exposing misinformation's motives*—In this lesson, students explore the various ways advertising plays a role in the dissemination of disinformation (Common Sense Education, n.d.). First, the lesson explains how advertisers and publishers make money through online advertising. Then, students explore the concept of *clickbait* and how fake news can become so profitable. As clickbait, featuring fake news articles becomes more profitable and the demand for creating these advertisements increases, leading to even more dissemination of fake news. A wrap-up Take a Stand activity involves a role-playing scenario during which students discuss the issue from various perspectives and brainstorm ways to combat the proliferation of fake news.

Analyzing Historical Sources

NewseumED (n.d.a) offers educators a high-quality collection of teaching materials meant to "cultivate the First Amendment and media literacy skills essential to civic life." Although the vast number of resources can seem overwhelming at first, the organization curates lessons and related resources into easy-to-comprehend collections, such as "Fact Finder: Your Foolproof Guide to Media Literacy" and "Making a Change: The First Amendment and the Civil Rights Movement." Each collection offers a variety of high-quality lesson plans and carefully aligned, primary-source documents. These collections also include an impressive number of engaging videos and other multimedia such as interactive timelines, maps, and quizzes (NewseumED, n.d.b).

- **Organization:** NewseumED
- **Grade range:** 3–12
- **Key topics:** News media literacy, First Amendment freedoms, civil rights, primary source analysis

Lesson spotlight: *Analyzing historical sources*—This lesson, as part of the "Media Literacy Booster Pack," exemplifies NewseumED's (n.d.c) ability to leverage its massive primary-source library to create a high-quality student experience. Over the course of the lesson, students use the ESCAPE acronym (evidence, sources, context, audience, purpose, execution) to analyze a variety of historical and contemporary examples of propaganda. Artifacts span topics from the Vietnam War of the 1960s, to women's suffrage during the later 1800s, to anti-Muslim sentiments of the early 2000s. The lesson also walks teachers through student discussion protocols with sample prompts to help students dive deeper into the issues and implications of modern-day propaganda (NewseumED, n.d.c).

Navigating Digital Information

MediaWise for Gen Z, an educational arm of the Poynter Institute, is designed to help teach "teens to be critical media consumers and make decisions based on facts" (Poynter, n.d.a). The program offers a variety of programs, such as their flagship Teen Fact-Checking Network (TFCN; Poynter, n.d.b). Conducted through social media channels such as Instagram and YouTube, TFCN designs content for a teen audience, hosted by students themselves. For example, a TFCN fact-check video "No, 5 UK Nurses Did Not Die From the COVID-19 Vaccine" (Kahkajian, 2021), hosted by a sixteen-year-old student, provides a thorough breakdown of false claims as well as a clear walkthrough of how she came to that conclusion.

- **Organization:** Poynter Institute
- **Grade range:** 6–12
- **Key topics:** Applying critical thinking to media consumption, and fact-based decision making

Lesson spotlight: *Navigating digital information*—Partnering with MediaWise and the Poynter Institute and Stanford History Education Project, author and YouTuber John Green, of the widely popular Crash Course (2020) education channel, developed a ten-part Navigating Digital Information series. In the video "Click Restraint," Green explains some of the underlying architecture of social media and searching, particularly how algorithms are designed to provide you with information that they deem most relevant and entertaining to you (Crash Course, 2019). This does not, in any way, mean that the information that appears first in your feed is the highest quality or most accurate information. Other helpful videos in this series include "Check Yourself With Lateral Reading," "Evaluating Photos and Videos," and "Data and Infographics" (Crash Course, 2020).

Understanding the Power of Images

The Democracy and Civic Engagement collection within the Facing History and Ourselves (n.d.b) archive aims to help students "investigate cornerstones of successful democracies, including religious freedom, a free press, media." Within this collection, media literacy features fifty-four resources that can be further refined by subject area (for example, civics, ELA, U.S. history) and resource type (for example, reading, lesson plan, teaching idea, video). One hallmark of the Facing History and Ourselves collection is its high-quality collection of current event resources that also make connections to historical events and trends throughout modern U.S. history. One example is the resource "What Happened During the Insurrection at the U.S. Capitol and Why?" (Facing History and Ourselves, 2021).

- **Organization:** Facing History and Ourselves
- **Grade range:** 3–12
- **Key topics:** Democracy and civic engagement, news media literacy

Lesson spotlight: *Understanding the power of images*—As part of the unit "Facing Ferguson: News Literacy in a Digital Age," The Power of Images lesson has students explore the power of imagery and how it can be interpreted differently based on people's backgrounds, life experiences, and existing biases (Facing History and Ourselves, n.d.c). After learning context behind race relations in Ferguson, Missouri, and the resulting protests, students examine how various news outlets portray the events through imagery. Students then engage in a simulation in which they play the role of editor that must determine which cover image should accompany the story. This experience then leads to a discussion around the role that imagery plays in reporting and consuming news media.

Tools to Enhance Online Research and Reasoning

Along with the quality curricular resources previously outlined, there are several powerful online tools that educators can leverage to enhance students' research and reasoning skills. These come in many forms, but typically fall within one of three categories: (1) quick quizzes and informal assessments to help students determine the nature of different sources or detect elements of bias; (2) resources and databases that help curate and categorize media outlets and current events based on their political leanings or style of presentation; and (3) online fact-checking resources that can serve as a tool in helping students evaluate the validity of information.

Pew Research Quiz

The Pew Research Center (2018b) quiz is a quick way for students to gauge their ability to distinguish factual news statements from opinion pieces. A sample statement to evaluate is *Increasing the federal minimum wage to $15 an hour is essential for the health of the U.S. economy*. Once complete, students can see how their results stack up when compared to over five thousand adults who took part in a national survey with the same questions (Pew Research Center, 2018b). (Visit www.pewresearch.org/quiz/news-statements-quiz to take the quiz, "How Well Can You Tell Factual From Opinion Statements?")

AllSides

AllSides (www.allsides.com) is a useful research platform that provides news stories that span the political spectrum. Although no platform can perfectly categorize each news story based on ideological leanings, the site does a good job of laying out key examples surrounding important stories of the day.

Not only can a platform like AllSides help students recognize political bias or ideological commentary based on news outlets, but it also can provide a valuable research tool for students to gain a deeper understanding of multiple perspectives on an issue.

Fact-Checking Tools

Another valuable research tool for students is a news media fact checker. Several are available, but we recommend the following two as the most reputable.

FactCheck.org

The first is FactCheck.org by the Annenberg Public Policy Center of the University of Pennsylvania. This nonprofit, nonpartisan group's mission involves "reducing the level of deception and confusion in U.S. politics through monitoring the factual accuracy of what is said by major U.S. political players in the form of TV ads, debates, speeches, interviews and news releases" (FactCheck.org, n.d.). What makes this platform useful is that it goes beyond simply calling out false claims. It also helps provide the reader with context regarding statements that are technically true but do not tell the whole story. For example, a FactCheck.org post highlights that although President Joe Biden's March 2021 statement that the United States would be the first nation in the world to vaccinate 100 million people, the implication that we are the world leader in vaccinations is misleading (Farley, 2021). In actuality, at the time Biden made this statement, the United States was fourth in vaccinations per capita, behind Israel, the United Arab Emirates, and the United Kingdom (Farley, 2021).

PolitiFact

A second reputable fact-checking site students can leverage for research is PolitiFact (politifact.com). Owned by the nonprofit Poynter Institute for Media

Studies, PolitiFact engages in a fact-checking process as an example of effective news media consumption that students could replicate. When fact-checking claims, students should consider the following (Holan, 2020):

- Is the statement rooted in a fact that is verifiable?
- Does the statement seem misleading or sound wrong?
- Is the statement significant?
- Is the statement likely to be passed on and repeated by others?
- Would a typical person hear or read the statement and wonder, "Is that true?"

Sound familiar? These are many of the same strategies taught in the news media literacy curriculum mentioned earlier in the chapter. This provides specific, real-world examples of these news media literacy strategies put into practice.

You may be thinking of various fact-checking websites you have come across that are biased themselves. And you are right; unfortunately, there are more biased fact checking sites than legitimate ones. As an educator, do not quickly dismiss these resources as useful since these biased fact checkers can be excellent teaching tools as well. For example, you can have students engage in a lesson that examines fact-checking from the website Media Matters, such as the report "COVID Misinformation, Racism, and Propaganda: Fox News' Newest Show Is Already a Disaster" (Sadowski & Martin, 2021). You can then have students examine fact checking from NewsBusters, such as the article "New MRC Poll PROVES Media's Cuomo Cover-Up Distorted Public's View" (NB Staff, 2021).

Hopefully, it wouldn't take students long to discover the ideological and political leanings for each organization that claims to be a fact checker and media watchdog. The key takeaway here for students is that just because a source may claim to be an unbiased organization that practices objective journalism, closer examination is often necessary to ensure the legitimacy of the source, or at least understand how bias and political ideology impact its reporting.

Conclusion

Teaching students how to combat misinformation and navigate an increasingly complex digital media landscape may be one of the most important tasks facing schools. We recognize that this is no easy endeavor. We hope that the resources and teaching strategies highlighted in this chapter will provide you with more practical tools and confidence to effectively engage in news media literacy lessons with students.

Key Takeaways for News Media Literacy for Combating Misinformation

Following are key takeaways from this chapter on news media literacy for combating misinformation.

- The increasing proliferation of fake, misleading, and biased information and news coverage is one of the core challenges facing democratic societies.
- Educators play a vital role in helping students develop the skills needed to discover and evaluate online information, and high-quality news media literacy programs are available to support them.
- Online research and fact-checking tools can help students navigate the complex and ever-changing world of digital news media.

Chapter 6

ENGAGEMENT THROUGH DIGITAL GAMES AND COMPETITIONS

Anyone who has spent time in the classroom understands the value of, and necessity for, student engagement. Without it, just about any lesson will fall flat. For students to truly understand something, particularly in a deeper way, their engagement in the learning process is essential. Educators understand that keeping students engaged may be more challenging than ever. That is precisely why the ability to leverage game competitions and showcases should be in every modern educator's repertoire.

In this chapter, we explore a variety of engaging civic education games and simulations that span topics such as constitutional law, news media literacy, and voting rights. All the games and simulations are easily accessible to students through a web browser, or in some cases, a free mobile app. We also explore high-quality programs that include student competitions and showcases as culminating events. Although there may be digital components to competitions or showcases, the idea is that students engage in some type of civics-related project and compete against other students from neighboring schools, or in some cases, across the United States and the world.

Digital Games

Gamification and game-based learning have become core tools in the modern educator's toolbox. Based on our experience working with teachers and schools across the nation, the adoption of one-on-one programs has accelerated the use of digital games and simulations in a variety of subject areas. Civic education is no exception. The following resources are what we consider the highest-quality civic education games and simulations currently implemented by educators. Each resource includes a brief description, grade range, and cost. For those resources that represent a large collection of games and simulations, we have also included a Lesson Spotlight highlighting one of our favorite resources from that platform.

iCivics

The standard-bearer for game-based civics simulations is iCivics (www.icivics.org). Founded by retired Supreme Court Justice Sandra Day O'Conner in 2009 to help reach a new generation of digitally savvy students, iCivics created a vast library of free online resources that are now used by over seven million students each year (iCivics, n.d.g). Among its most popular resources is a series of engaging civics video games that provide simulated experiences such as running a constitutional law firm (Do I Have a Right?), growing a social media news site (NewsFeed Defenders), and running a successful political campaign (Win the White House; iCivics, n.d.e).

- **Grade range:** 3–12
- **Key topics:** U.S. Constitution, U.S. history, civil rights, state and local government, politics and public policy, citizenship and civic action, news media literacy
- **Cost:** Free

Lesson spotlight: *Cast your vote*—For educators, iCivics provides a thorough teacher resource guide that includes suggested activities, resources, and classroom conversation starters. Suggested prompts include "What was your strategy to become a prepared voter?" and "Which [propositions] might be seen in a community like yours?" (iCivics, n.d.a).

Games for Change

Another powerful collection of digital games and simulations is curated by the organization Games for Change. Established in 2004 to "empower game creators and social innovators to drive real-world change using games and immersive media," this resource has proven valuable for educators that seek impactful student experiences related to their curriculum area, particularly classes that explore civic issues (Games for Change, n.d.a). The game archive is designed so educators can easily search by age range as well as a variety of topics, such as civics, history, environmentalism, politics, conflict, and empathy (Games for Change, n.d.d).

- **Grade range:** K–12
- **Key topics:** Civics, history, politics
- **Cost:** Most are free (cost for others varies).

Lesson spotlight: *Fake it to make it*—This lesson can appear somewhat controversial at first. The premise of the game is that players assume the role of a company that creates and spreads fabricated news articles as part of its business model. As the players progress, they receive challenges that lead them to create "politically-divided sites, selecting articles that inspire negative emotions like fear and anger, and distributing their articles to politically sympathetic groups" (Games for Change, n.d.c).

Although teaching students how to create and distribute fake news may seem counterintuitive, the goal of this simulation is to help students gain knowledge of the process and drivers of fake news. This deeper understanding can help students better identify fake news in the real world and "generate healthy skepticism" regarding news media that show evidence of fabrication (Games for Change, n.d.c).

Factitious

Created by a team of researchers at the American University (n.d.) Game Lab, Factitious is a collection of games that test your ability to identify fake news stories (Factitious, n.d.). The 2018 version includes six game modes based on difficulty and reading level and quickly racked up over one million gameplays (Hone, 2018). The game mechanics are simple—students swipe the article to the right if they think it is real news and to the left if they think it is fake news. An updated Pandemic Edition was released in 2020 to focus on news stories related to the coronavirus and vaccine development (Factitious, n.d.).

- **Grade range:** 6–12
- **Key topics:** News media literacy
- **Cost:** Free

Informable

Created by the News Literacy Project, Informable is an iOS and Android app designed to test students' ability to discern fact from fiction across various platforms (https://informable.newslit.org). More specifically, the game aims to teach students how to distinguish information related to the following four categories: "news articles from opinion pieces, advertisements from other types of information, false evidence from sound evidence, and fact-based statements from opinion-based statements" (Apple App Store, n.d.). After mastering the various levels, students encounter the mix-up mode, which provides a more real-world experience with less guidance and scaffolding from the app.

- **Grade range:** 6–12
- **Key topics:** News media literacy
- **Cost:** Free

Lives in the Balance (iThrive Games)

In a game developed with support of the National Endowment for the Humanities, students receive the following challenge: "How do you make critical governmental decisions when time is of the essence and the information you rely on is constantly changing?" (iThrive Games, n.d.). Based on a not-so-far-fetched scenario of government officials grappling with how to manage their state during a virus outbreak, students are tasked with navigating conflicting information, taking and defending positions, engaging in compromise, and forming coalitions. Some of the key activities students engage with in this simulation include making informed decisions based on data, weighing competing priorities, and considering federal versus states' rights.

- **Grade range:** 6–12
- **Key topics:** Public policy, data analysis, complex decision making, state and local government
- **Cost:** Free

In helping to discover how educators can use games to engage students, we conducted the following interview with Anahita Dalmia, chief executive officer of Alterea, an award-winning, immersive experience design company moving students from passive entertainment (listening to a story) to becoming part of the action (living the story). Her team is currently developing the game Agents of Influence, focusing on online research, critical reading, analysis, and persuasion.

These resources represent the highest-quality civic education games available to educators. More are undoubtedly on the horizon, as evident in our discussion with the developer of the upcoming Agents of Influence. Explore these resources to see what is the best fit for you and your students, while also keeping an eye out for even more engaging games and simulations to come aimed at enhancing civic education.

> **Interview With Anahita Dalmia**
> **About the Game Agents of Influence**
>
> *Q: What knowledge and skills do you hope to help build with your project?*
>
> A: The core objectives are to test the trustworthiness of information by using a healthier dose of skepticism and investigation of information (for example, asking the right questions, analyzing research and comparing resources, and coming to logical conclusions). We also want to help with specific skills such as how to use search tools effectively, recognize bias, identify different types of sources, and discern fact from opinion. The goal is to use this knowledge to make better decisions, and to understand that the decisions you make have consequences.
>
> *Q: Why do you find these skills and competencies so important?*
>
> A: The problem of misinformation has been around since civilization began. The current issue is that the digital age has expedited the spread of misinformation exponentially. This proliferation of misinformation takes away people's agency. The decisions made and actions taken by citizens over the past several years have mattered more than ever. These decisions then lead to the establishment of a new normal. Misinformation disempowers people and makes them vulnerable. They end up making decisions that do not align with their ideals. (A. Dalmia, personal communication, August 20, 2021)

Competitions

Of course, not all games and simulations need to be conducted through digital media such as those highlighted earlier. In fact, some of the most powerful experiences are facilitated through live student competitions and showcases taking place each year across the United States and the world. Let's turn to the most popular, reputable, and up-and-coming programs available to educators.

We the People: Mock Congressional Hearing Competition

One of the most popular and effective civic education programs is the Center for Civic Education's "We the People: The Citizen and the Constitution" (Center for Civic Education, n.d.b). (The curriculum is available at www.civiced.org/we-the-people, in both print and online versions.) The culminating activity of this curriculum is its simulated congressional hearing competition (Center for Civic Education, n.d.b). Although teachers can opt for non-competitive experiences, many schools from around the United States enter their classes into state-level competitions. A team of volunteer judges scores students based on criteria such as reasoning, constitutional application, and supporting evidence (Center for Civic Education, n.d.a).

Each year, state winning teams are then eligible to compete in the national finals in the Washington, D.C., area.

As a participant in the national competition representing Rhode Island (West Warwick High School), Tom can attest to the powerful impact that this experience can have on students. In more quantifiable terms, a team of researchers from Georgetown University found that students who participated in the We the People competition "scored significantly higher on tests of both civic knowledge and civic dispositions than their peers" (Center for Civic Education, n.d.c).

> **We the People: Mock Congressional Hearing Competition**
>
> The We the People: Mock Congressional Hearing incorporates so many essential skills students need. For example, researching information, analyzing it, then developing a strong, evidence-based argument. It also puts them in situations in which they will have to defend a position that they don't necessarily agree with, which requires tons of critical thinking. The questions asked also have a lot of connections to their own lives as they grapple with issues affecting their own experiences and people around them (for example, how Supreme Court cases affect their rights as students).
>
> The live performance task and being able to perform on the spot were a great experience for kids. There was pressure, but in a good way. It pushes kids to think critically and do it quickly on their feet. This process also shows depth of knowledge as students have to justify their answers using primary sources and an understanding of historical precedents. (M. LeBlanc, social studies teacher and department head at West Warwick High School in Rhode Island; personal communication, August 13, 2021)

Generation Citizen Civics Day Competition

Generation Citizen is all about action civics. The Civics Day event is a chance for students involved in the program to share their action civics proposals with an authentic audience. Typically conducted both in the fall and spring, Civics Day events can be considered a science fair for civics that brings together local officials and community leaders to hear students' ideas, engage in dialogue, and provide feedback and insights (Generation Citizen, n.d.b).

Project Soapbox

Facilitated by the Mikva Challenge (n.d.b), an action civics–style program referenced in chapter 3 (page 33), Project Soapbox is a public speaking competition that "calls young people to speak out on issues that affect them and their communities." In the first stage, students must identify an issue they care about, engage in research, and craft a two-minute speech with a clear call to action. At the school level, students deliver their speeches to peers and, in some cases, hold schoolwide events. The next stage is a citywide event during which school-based representatives present their speeches. The final stage is a national showcase called Soapbox Nation, featuring twelve finalists who are invited to a virtual mainstage event (Mikva Challenge, n.d.d).

Kidizenship Competitions

A relatively new organization, Kidizenship (n.d.a), has developed a media platform designed to merge "civic education with creative self-expression and community action." It offers a series of contests open to students ages 8–18, including cash prizes for the top three winners in each category (Kidizenship, n.d.b). The Fly Your Flag competition invites students to create their own version of the American flag using a medium of their choice. The Write Your Hero contest asks students to write about someone they believe exemplifies American ideals. Make Your Speech asks for two- to three-minute videos of students who role-play their first speech as president, outlining their vision for the future of the United States. Other contests include Sing Your Anthem, Champion Your Cause, and Build Your Monument.

Games for Change (G4C) Student Competition

Organized by the Games for Change (n.d.e) organization discussed earlier, the G4C Student Challenge competition is designed to "combine students' passion for games with digital learning and civic engagement." Three main elements to the program reach thousands of students each year. First, it provides professional development for teachers who conduct the game design courses. Second, it offers a set of social impact themes to "elevate civic engagement, ignite curiosity and inspire students to research and design original impact games" (Games for Change, n.d.e). Third, it provides full game-design courses to help students put their ideas into action. G4C holds an annual competition organized for students to share their games and compete with other students for prizes and scholarship opportunities.

A specific example is the Build a Better World competition in which the game design prompt is to "create a game that celebrates diversity and teaches people how to uplift marginalized voices" (Games for Change, n.d.b).

Conclusion

Digital games and competitions have long been leveraged by educators to enhance student engagement and provide more authenticity to the learning experience. Fortunately, since 2009, there has been a proliferation of high-quality digital games aimed at civics instruction. From the reputable library of iCivics games to the emerging apps aimed at teaching news media literacy, educators have more options than ever. There are also many opportunities for students to engage in regional and national competitions and showcases, such as Generation Citizen's Civics Day, We the People's Mock Congressional Hearings, and Kidizenship's recurring contests. We strongly encourage you to add civics-related digital games and competitions to your teaching toolbox.

Key Takeaways for Engagement Through Digital Games and Competitions

Following are key takeaways from this chapter on engagement through digital games and competitions.

- ▸ Digital games and student competitions can increase motivation and engagement in civic education experiences.

- ▸ Digital games and simulations of civics experiences provide teachers with more versatility in crafting and implementing civics lessons.

- ▸ Competitions and student showcases, such as Generation Citizen's Civics Day and the Mikva Challenge's Soapbox Nation, provide students with opportunities to collaborate and share ideas with a wider audience through real-world experiences.

PART 3

CIVICS LESSONS ACROSS SUBJECT AREAS

Chapter 7

CIVICS LESSONS FOR SOCIAL STUDIES

Even though civics instruction is already part of the social studies curriculum, a key part of meaningful reform of civic education is a shift to creating meaningful experiences and using high-quality simulations. The following two lessons model these important shifts. Take a moment to consider how much time students will spend engaging in each of the lessons in this chapter. The excitement of discovery adds a lot of energy to a lesson.

In the lecture model, teachers share information with their students and only then ask them to engage in any form of work. Unfortunately, that has the effect of taking away any surprise or excitement about reaching the end of the process because they know where the activity is going. Watching a movie in which you already know the ending changes the experience because the surprise is gone. Telling students the outcome before they have a chance to explore affects them in a similar way.

In this chapter, we explore two original sample lessons for social studies, including both elementary and secondary levels. Though civics is already included in most social studies classes, these lessons seek to provide opportunities for students to engage with the mechanisms of democracy, communicate with leaders in their community, and participate in civil discourse. For each lesson, we include the grade range, topics, standards connections (both U.S. and Canadian), civics connections, time frame, lesson overview and implementation steps, and a sample lesson in action to illustrate how it might play out in a classroom setting. Following each lesson is a list of go-to resources to help you implement and enrich each lesson.

These are, of course, just a starting point that hopefully will offer a spark of inspiration for teachers looking to authentically weave civics into their social studies lessons. Let your own creativity guide you in making connections between your content area and real-world scenarios that involve aspects of public life.

Elementary Social Studies Lesson

This lesson focuses on having the class identify a need that exists within the community. It begins with students generating a list. Student groups then research each of the identified issues and, as a class, decide which community service goal to pursue. Students develop a plan to address their chosen problem and seek to enact it.

Leaders in Our Community

- **Grade range:** 3–5
- **Topics:** Action civics, service learning, research
- **Social studies standards connections:**
  - *D2. Civ. 6.3–5*—Describe ways in which people benefit from and are challenged by working together, including through government, workplaces, voluntary organizations, and families (National Council for the Social Studies [NCSS], 2013).
  - *D2. Civ. 7.3–5*—Apply civic virtues and democratic principles in school settings (NCSS, 2013).
  - *D2. Civ. 13.3–5*—Explain how policies are developed to address public problems (NCSS, 2013).
  - *B2*—Use the social studies inquiry process to investigate Canadian social and environmental issues from various perspectives, including those of Indigenous peoples as well as of the level (or levels) of government responsible for addressing the issue (Ontario Ministry of Education, 2018).
- **Civics connections:** Students learn how to work toward a goal, address community needs, and inform local leaders. They gain experience accessing the democratic process to reach their objective.

▸ **Time frame:** Three to four hours of initial class time (length and duration of the activity will vary based on the project selected by the class)

Lesson Overview

Organize the class to identify a need that exists within the community. Groups of students can research each of the identified issues and, as a class, decide which community service goal to pursue. Students will develop a plan to address their chosen problem. Work with the class to engage local leaders in the discussion as well as develop a plan to educate community members about the problem. The class will discuss which local leaders have jurisdiction and, therefore, the power to resolve the issue. Once students have executed their plan, they will reflect on what they learned by participating in the process.

1. Students examine issues that exist within the community. Help them understand the issues more thoroughly and identify key issues at the core of each problem.

2. Students work in groups to research the problem and determine possible solutions. Informed by their research, they select one topic relevant to them to pursue together over the course of the year.

3. Once they select their topic, students can use a design process (such as the design thinking model found at https://dschool.stanford.edu/resources/getting-started-with-design-thinking) to develop a strategy and plan of action. They determine which public officials they need to contact and how they can build public support. Students may decide to attend and speak at local government meetings to make their case and generate interest in their plan.

4. Upon successful (or unsuccessful) completion of the plan, students reflect on what they learned, what steps they took to be successful, and how they might have done things differently if given the chance.

Extension Activity

Consider having students share the story of their project with other classes. Ask them to research other groups currently working to enact change. Ask students to look at proposed reforms that did *not* succeed and analyze why they may not have been successful.

Sample Lesson in Action

Mr. Thomas wants to create a meaningful experience for his grade 4 students that involves contributing to the community. He decides that the best way to make it meaningful for his students is to allow them to work together to pick a class project they could work on throughout the school year. He asks students to brainstorm issues that exist in the community. He begins by asking students to interview their parents and family members to find out about the needs and problems in the community. Students create a class list of what they learn. Many issues focus on the environment or school. One student, Rebecca, wins over the rest of the class by identifying that many residents of the nearby Fair Oaks Senior Community have no relatives or visitors. Rebecca wonders if there is a way to do something for them.

The students embrace the idea and start looking at how they can make a difference. Mr. Thomas reaches out to the director of Fair Oaks Senior Community and invites her to be a guest speaker. The students ask questions about the residents' needs, list ideas, and vote on a plan to include Fair Oaks residents in the Mystery Reader program at the school. Mr. Thomas explains that the principal would need to approve the plan, so he asks students to write letters to state their case. When the letters are ready, Mr. Thomas asks a small group of students to deliver the letters to the main office. Principal Benjamin comes to the class to approve the plan.

After several weeks, residents of Fair Oaks write thank you notes to the class. At the conclusion of the reading program, students express interest in continuing to help the residents. The class returns to their list and identifies the difficulty residents have when traveling the short distance to the school. The students decide that they will try to get upgraded ramps installed on the sidewalk so more Fair Oaks residents can get to the school. Students research the cost of the project, learn the process for getting the work approved, and create a script for the city council meeting. The students share their cost research and highlight the number of residents who would benefit from the ramps. They write letters to follow up with the city council and create a class Twitter account to share their work with the public.

The class cheers when they hear that the plan has been approved and funded by the city. Mr. Thomas is excited about his students' commitment to the work throughout the year but even happier that they learned so much about what it takes to create meaningful change and serve the community.

Go-To Resources

Following are valuable resources to enrich this lesson and engage students.

- Ideo is a leader in design thinking. Its resources are free to share. The focus is not education, but its blog upacks concepts in a way that will help you become knowledgeable (https://designthinking.ideo.com).

- The Stanford design school has resources to get you started using design thinking with students. This resource provides several models as well as a facilitator's guide that is great for modeling lessons of your own.
    - Stanford d.school Design Thinking website (https://dschool.stanford.edu/resources/getting-started-with-design-thinking)
    - Stanford d.school Design Thinking facilitator's guide (https://dschool.stanford.edu/s/Facilitators-Guide_Design-Thinking.pdf)
- The Constitutional Rights Foundation's Civic Action Project has high-quality examples of class projects. Shared via short videos, it is a good place to imagine the possibilities and get excited about a civic action project of your own (https://crfcap.org/mod/page/view.php?id=231#filter-tabs-content-1-2).
- The "Lessons on Local Government" website has a rich collection of resources specifically for younger students (www.lessonsonlocalgovernment.org/online-activities).

Secondary Social Studies Lesson

This lesson focuses on an aspect of the electoral process that can be hard to understand but is crucial to understanding the concept of representation. Instead of a lecture, this lesson asks students to actually perform gerrymandering on a hypothetical district. Students can choose the party for which they want to perform the gerrymander, which gives them an opportunity to see each of the gerrymandering tactics in use.

Gerrymandering in the United States: Curse or Blessing?

- **Grade range:** 10–12
- **Topics:** Gerrymandering, reapportioning, and redistricting; packing, cracking, and kidnapping; equal representation; one person, one vote
- **Social studies standards connections:**
    - *D2. Civ. 4.9–12*—Explain how the U.S. Constitution establishes a system of government that has powers, responsibilities, and limits that have changed over time and that are still contested (NCSS, 2013).
    - *D2. Civ. 8.9–12*—Evaluate social and political systems in different contexts, times, and places, that promote civic virtues and enact democratic principles (NCSS, 2013).

› *D2. Civ. 12.9–12*—Analyze how people use and challenge local, state, national, and international laws to address a variety of public issues (NCSS, 2013).

› *E1: Influence, Power, and Decision Making*—Demonstrate an understanding of how power is distributed and exercised in Canada and other countries, and of factors that affect its distribution (Ontario Ministry of Education, 2015).

▸ **Social studies connections:** Students will understand how citizens are represented in government and how redistricting and gerrymandering can affect that representation.

▸ **Time frame:** Three to four hours

Lesson Overview

Students participate in a virtual gerrymandering simulation to learn what gerrymandering is and how politicians use it to gain power and ensure political control. Rather than learn simple vocabulary, students apply the concepts of *packing* (combining all voters of an opposing party into one district to weaken its influence in other districts), *cracking* (spreading out voters of one party to reduce its voters to a minority in a district), and *kidnapping* (redistricting a district specifically to exclude an elected representative so he or she does not meet the residency requirement to run again) to a virtual congressional district (Pierce, Larson, & Beckett, 2011). Once they complete the simulation, students share an image of their gerrymandered district so the class can review how widely redistricting can vary. The class then explores the origins of redistricting law via the Constitution, court cases, and laws. Next, students prepare a position statement on gerrymandering that they will use to guide their participation in a structured debate to answer the question, *Is gerrymandering in America a powerful way to make sure power is redistributed over time to reflect the changing population, or a negative way to manipulate power and deny people their rights?*

1. Students complete several challenges within the Redistricting Game (www.redistrictinggame.org). After completing each challenge, they take a screenshot of their map and submit it via a Google Form. Ask students to balance out a district to equalize populations. They then try to gerrymander the district to create a political advantage for the party of their choosing. Students will learn about packing, cracking, and kidnapping in context through several challenges. After completing each challenge, they take a screenshot of their solution and submit it for class analysis.

2. Share students' screenshots with the class, and ask students to compare the different districts that were created. Students will analyze the dramatic differences that are possible. The class then discusses the implications of such differences on voting and elections.

> **Teacher Tip: Show, Don't Tell**
>
> Once students have turned in a product, it's tempting to turn your mind to grading it. With these gerrymander examples, it would be powerful to simply show the products to the class and ask students what they notice. In addition to building analytical skills, learning from student products means that students are creating class materials that tangibly affect learning. Students will want to make sure their work is included, and this can cause completion rates to increase.
>
> Use a Google Drive or OneDrive® to collect and share these artifacts. It increases interest and engages their curiosity about how others solved the challenge. (See an example student sharing slide deck by visiting https://bit.ly/36OO14N.)

3. Having experienced how people can use redistricting for equality but also for political advantage, students explore the origin of the rules for redistricting by researching the Permanent Apportionment Act of 1929 (U.S. House of Representatives, n.d.) or the *Wesberry v. Sanders* case summary (www.oyez.org/cases/1963/22). This case established that congressional districts should have equal populations.

4. Using their experience in the simulation and the knowledge gained from research, students write a position statement in response to the prompt, *Is gerrymandering in America a powerful way to make sure power is redistributed over time to reflect the changing population, or a negative way to manipulate power and deny people their rights?* Students are welcome to reject both options to create a view of their own outside of this binary.

5. Students use their position statements to contribute to a structured debate. Students take turns sharing their statements, and then the class can submit questions to a class moderator, who shares them with the speaker for a response. After the class has finished sharing, students can revise their position statements before finally submitting them to you.

Extension Activity

Students can reach out to state legislators to share their insight into gerrymandering and suggest reforms, emphasizing the evidence that led them to their informed

Chapter 8
CIVICS LESSONS FOR ENGLISH LANGUAGE ARTS

Much like reading and writing skills, civic education need not be confined to one class. Ideally, responsibility for civic education will not rest solely with social studies teachers or civics classes. Subject-area teachers can begin incorporating civics by addressing current events within the context of their subject area or by prioritizing skills that are essential to becoming an informed and discerning citizen. There can be a benefit to teaching such skills independent of politics and government. If the whole school has a vision of the student as a citizen and the responsibility for socializing belongs to the entire staff, it is more likely that these skills and values will take root.

Incorporating civics into ELA does not mean that the curriculum needs to be put on pause for an overt civics lesson. The idea is to embed key skills and civic dispositions into lessons where they exist in context. It might mean allowing one of the enrichment choices to focus on an area of government in the community. ("Write a letter to someone in your community sharing your opinion.") It might be one station in a station-rotation activity. ("In station two, you will read the works of prominent journalists calling on the government to act.") It might mean not changing anything in a lesson but taking the time to identify a role of government in close proximity to the topic for the day. ("Yes, that is correct; this book is from 2015. How did you determine that? Oh, you used the copyright date? That's correct. A copyright is issued by the government in order to protect the intellectual property of the author. The year of the book will always be listed.") The following lessons emphasize the connection between civic skills and dispositions and the ELA classroom.

These are, of course, just a starting point and hopefully a spark of inspiration for teachers looking to authentically weave civics into their ELA lessons. Let your own creativity guide you in making connections between your content area and real-world scenarios that involve aspects of public life.

Elementary English Language Arts Lesson

The important skill in this lesson is the concept of identifying fact and opinion statements. It is important to democracy that citizens are informed and able to discern facts. This lesson aims to have students explore fact and opinion and teaches them a variety of ways to evaluate a text.

Opinion Writing and Revising for the Effective Use of Supporting Facts

- **Grade range:** 3–5
- **Topics:** Opinion writing, constructing informed opinions, identifying opinion statements, evaluating facts to construct opinions
- **ELA standards connections:**
  - *W.4.1*—Write opinion pieces on topics or texts, supporting a point of view with reasons and information (National Governors Association Center for Best Practices [NGA] & Council of Chief State School Officers [CCSSO], 2010a).
  - *W.4.1b*—Provide reasons that are supported by facts and details (NGA & CCSSO, 2010a).
  - *W.4.1d*—Provide a concluding statement or section related to the opinion presented (NGA & CCSSO, 2010a).
  - *Purpose and Audience 1.1*—Identify the topic, purpose, and audience for a variety of writing forms (Ontario Ministry of Education, 2006).
  - *Analyzing Texts 1.7*—Analyze texts and explain how specific elements in them contribute to meaning (Ontario Ministry of Education, 2006).

- **Civics connections:** The ability to identify statements of opinion and statements of fact within written statements and the ability to use facts to construct informed opinions are key to being an informed and responsible citizen.
- **Time frame:** Two to three hours (depending on whether the writing portion is done during or outside of class time)

Lesson Overview

During step one of the lesson, students write an opinion essay informed by researched facts. They then examine the essays written by classmates to identify opinion and fact statements. In the last part of the activity, students apply their skills to a series of opinion articles. Working in groups, they first identify fact- and opinion-based statements and then discuss the statements they identified in small groups.

1. Begin the lesson by sharing several fact and opinion statements with the class. Ask students to identify which statements are facts and which are opinions. Have students discuss how they determined their answers and create a list of strategies. You might collect these fact and opinion statements from student council materials within your own school or from articles published about your school in the local press.

2. Share a selection of opinion adjectives and fact adjectives that students can use to identify fact and opinion statements in the next activity (see figure 8.1, page 100).

3. Have students practice creating fact and opinion statements by writing three factual statements and three opinion statements of their own. Then lead the class in share-outs. As students share their statements, direct them back to the guide to identify what makes each statement a fact or an opinion. An alternate activity for older students would be to use the PolitiFact website (politifact.com) to make a collection of fact and fiction statements made by public officials to use in the activity. These could be passed out and shared together with the statements that students create.

4. Extend the lesson by asking students to write a short paragraph about one of their opinions using supporting facts.

5. Students share their paragraphs with a classmate and use the guide to identify fact and opinion statements within their partner's paragraph. Allow them to discuss their opinions and identify where their opinions differ. This is a key aspect of healthy civil discourse.

Opinion Adjectives	Fact Adjectives
best	**Specific Amounts**
worst	many
better than	few
worse than	ten
most	more than
least	**Specific Sizes**
terrible	big
amazing	little
cool	green
attractive	gold
beautiful	blue
ugly	yellow
gross	round
strange	flat
wonderful	oblong
interesting	**Shapes and Colors**
boring	large
	small
	tallest
	shortest
	Specific Materials
	paper
	plastic
	wooden
Tip: Sometimes people use more than one adjective to describe something. Usually, but not always, when they do, they use the opinion adjective first, followed by the fact adjective. *The cute little cottage* *The beautiful stone statue*	

Source: Cambridge Dictionary, *n.d.*

Figure 8.1: Opinion and fact adjectives.

6. Students can use their paragraph to share an opinion about the school with the administration. (Public schools are a function of government.) Tell students that you will deliver their writing in person; this adds weight and importance to the assignment. You might invite the principal to visit the classroom and listen to students. The principal

might be able to identify some things they can implement or correct. (For example: "Marcelino shared that the ground at the bottom of the slide was rocky and someone might get hurt. I am going to make sure that we fix that surface so all of you are safe when you play," and "Farheen mentioned that sometimes her dad is not able to come to the monthly awards program and asked if it could be in the morning. That's a great idea, Farheen! I'm going to look into having some of the award ceremonies in the morning before school so your dad can see you and be proud!")

Extension Activity

In the days and weeks ahead, ask students to apply their skills using leveled current events articles from Newsela (https://newsela.com) or News in Levels (www.newsinlevels.com). Once they have developed proficiency in identifying fact and opinion statements within articles, you can begin to discuss the effectiveness of the articles and develop future lessons that evaluate arguments made in opinion writing.

Sample Lesson in Action

To kick off the fifth-grade unit on opinion writing, Ms. Meierding displays ten statements on her SMART Board:

1. Attending college will result in you earning more money on average than people who do not.
2. The Chicago Cubs are the best team in professional baseball.
3. Women are often paid less than men who work in similar jobs.
4. Crocodiles are uncommon in the United States.
5. It does not make sense to live in a state where tornadoes occur.
6. It is harder to learn to play the drums than it is to learn to play guitar.
7. Mathematics is more important than science.
8. Women have a longer life expectancy than men.
9. The moon is much smaller than the Earth.
10. All cats are more friendly than dogs.

She tells the class that some of the statements are facts and some are opinions. She asks students to read and identify them, and then come to the board and drag the sentences to the correct columns where they belong.

Once students have correctly organized the statements, Ms. Meierding asks them how they were able to determine fact from opinion. She documents their responses to create a class list.

- Opinion statements have pronouns like *I*, *me*, *we*, and *they*. Personal pronouns can mean it's a personal opinion.
- Factual statements have very specific facts that can be checked to make sure they are true.
- Words like *always*, *everyone*, and *never* usually mean a statement is an opinion.
- Fact statements are easy to point out because I ask myself, "Where could I look for that?," and I can come up with something. Opinion statements are like talking to my uncle. He might believe what he says, but the rest of the family does not agree.

Ms. Meierding follows up the discussion by sharing her guide to fact and opinion adjectives. Students review the resource to evaluate the list the class generated and add to it. Students are excited that their list matches some of the information on Ms. Meierding's list. Students complete part one of the activity by writing three fact statements and three opinion statements of their own. Ms. Meierding asks students to share their statements and challenges the class to classify each one.

The next day, Ms. Meierding tells students that they will be writing opinion paragraphs. Each paragraph needs to be supported by factual statements. Jeremy writes an essay stating that the Chicago Cubs are the best professional baseball team in the world, using historical win-loss records and attendance data he finds online. Camden writes an essay describing why the musical *Hamilton* (Miranda, 2016) is the best Broadway show ever written, citing a book from the classroom library that lists box office records and citing awards won. When finished, Ms. Meierding assigns students partners. Partners review each other's paragraphs using the class-created strategy resource and identify fact and opinion statements. Later, Ms. Meierding shares leveled current events readings as a bell-ringer activity to refine students' skills.

> **Teacher Tip: Student-Created Learning Experiences**
>
> In some cases, when students use materials created by peers, they are more open to learning. And if students are excited about a task, they will invest energy into it. You may use tools like Kahoot! (https://kahoot.com), Quizizz (https://quizizz.com), and Socrative (www.socrative.com) to help students build learning experiences for each other. Use these experiences for students who need extra support or as bell-ringer activities.

Go-To Resources

Following are valuable resources to enrich this lesson and engage students.

- News Literacy Project (https://newslit.org)
- Facing History and Ourselves (www.facinghistory.org)
- Newsela (https://newsela.com)
- News in Levels (www.newsinlevels.com)
- Literacy Ideas (www.literacyideas.com)
- PolitiFact (www.politifact.com)

Secondary English Language Arts Lesson

In a democratic society, winning an election means influencing or responding to the opinions of the electorate. Citizens who address the government for the redress of their grievances need to convince others to join them in their efforts. In a democracy, influencing people is key to the system working effectively. The natural connection between rhetoric and government makes for natural connections within the ELA curriculum. This lesson explores both the ways leaders try to influence their constituents as well as the ways citizens reach out to influence their elected officials.

The Power of Persuasion: Advocating for Change in the World

- **Grade range:** 10–11
- **Topics:** Rhetorical devices, rhetorical appeals, visualization techniques, oral speeches
- **ELA standards connections:**
  - *W.4.1*—Write opinion pieces on topics or texts, supporting a point of view with reasons and information (NGA & CCSSO, 2010a).
  - *W.4.1a*—Introduce a topic or text clearly, state an opinion, and create an organizational structure in which related ideas are grouped to support the writer's purpose (NGA & CCSSO, 2010a).
  - *W.4.3d*—Use concrete words and phrases and sensory details to convey experiences and events precisely (NGA & CCSSO, 2010a).
  - *W.4.4*—Produce clear and coherent writing in which the development and organization are appropriate to task, purpose, and

audience (grade-specific expectations for writing types are defined previously in standards 1–3; NGA & CCSSO, 2010a).

- **Civics connections:** Writing and delivering persuasive speeches; analyzing historical speeches and evaluating persuasive rhetoric; writing persuasive letters
- **Time frame:** Two to three hours

Lesson Overview

Begin the unit by asking students for examples of how people try to influence them in their daily lives and then some ways they try to influence other people in their lives. Building on this conversation, the class explores some of the early American persuasive writing with Jonathan Edwards's (Edwards & Smolinski, 1741) "Sinners in the Hands of an Angry God." The class then chooses from a selection of famous speeches by contemporary American leaders and repeats the process of analyzing the speeches in small groups.

Discuss how although the sermon was a leader trying to influence people, in a democracy it is the responsibility of the people to influence their leaders. The next task is for each student to create a persuasive essay to be delivered either to the class or shared with the community in a way that can influence opinions or public policy.

1. Ask students who is trying to influence them in their daily lives. As the class shares, ask a student to document the conversation to create a list, asking, "Who is doing it, and what are they trying to get you to do?" After creating the list, share that you will explore the concept of persuasion so students will be able to identify efforts to persuade them and be able to better convey their beliefs and persuade others.

2. Have students evaluate Edwards's sermon "Sinners in the Hands of an Angry God" (Edwards & Smolinski, 1741). Give each student a copy of the essay for annotation and play audio selections from YouTube (www.youtube.com/watch?v=3vmvZIAGKJo) of the essay so the class can hear it delivered in the format for which it was intended.

3. Divide the class into groups, and assign each group a small section of the essay. Have students look for the author's purpose, persuasive devices, similes, metaphors, and powerful visualizations within the essay. Then have them share parts of the essay they feel were most effective as well as the devices that made them so.

4. Offer students a selection of famous political oratories, or allow them to choose from politicians or activists whom they admire. Using opposing

pieces allows students to compare, contrast, and process differing arguments. Working in their groups, students analyze the speeches and essays, sharing strong examples from each to a class Google Form where they can collect examples as a class resource to reference in the future.

5. Discuss how although the speeches and sermons discussed so far were leaders trying to influence people, in a democracy it is the responsibility of the people to influence their leaders.

6. To conclude this lesson, ask each student to create an individual persuasive essay to deliver either to the class or share with the community in a way that can influence opinions or public policy.

Extension Activity

Work with students to determine how to best share their persuasive work for its intended purpose. Knowing this should influence how students write their essays. It might be best for some to present at local government meetings or the city council, school board, park district, and so on. You might invite students to share their work with groups or elected officials via social media. Others might find an audience in community groups. In cases where no clear forum exists, you can create opportunities with school leadership or student groups. Focus on people or places where the class might influence public opinion and elected government officials to effect real change. The class might decide to select and pursue a smaller number of these issues to commit more effort to a more specific cause.

Sample Lesson in Action

Ms. Jackson wants the unit on persuasion to be more meaningful and personal to students. It is important that students can identify persuasive techniques and be aware of societal efforts to influence them. Ms. Jackson plans to build on required texts within the curriculum by allowing students to choose modern speeches and essays for analysis and discussion within their critical thinking groups. After analyzing two standard Puritan sermons for the author's purpose, persuasive devices, similes, metaphors, and powerful visualizations, and then reviewing more modern persuasive speeches, Ms. Jackson asks students to write their own brief persuasive essay, which they will workshop in small groups in which they proofread for each other and provide each other with feedback on how they can be more persuasive. She wants students to have experience sharing their work in meaningful ways.

As a final step, students break into small groups to make suggestions for where they could share each essay to have its desired effect or to influence public opinion. To provide the class with a meaningful experience, Ms. Jackson has the class select two local issues and work to bring the issues to the attention of local voters. One group presents to the school board to seek more funding for updated and timely elective classes, while another presents a plan to the city council requesting the creation of a youth advisory committee to advocate for student-centered improvements to public spaces, such as lockers for backpacks and more bike racks.

Go-To Resources

Following are valuable resources to enrich this lesson and engage students.

- American Rhetoric's list of the 100 greatest American speeches (www.americanrhetoric.com/top100speechesall.html)

- USA.gov is an official government website that helps identify your federal, state, and local elected officials (www.usa.gov/elected-officials).

- If your curriculum has a broader world focus, you can access historical speeches from across the world at The History Place™: Great Speeches Collection (www.historyplace.com/speeches/previous.htm).

Conclusion

Because of the important relationship between political influence and written and spoken communication, you can build many bridges between civics and ELA. Without the ability to critically evaluate rhetoric, citizens will struggle to discern truth and evaluate well-crafted speeches. Without this knowledge, they will be limited in the way that they can express their views and gather support to influence the political process and even democracy itself.

Key Takeaways for Civics Lessons for English Language Arts

Following are key takeaways from this chapter on civics lessons for ELA.

- As a key to winning elections or influencing others to join your cause, political rhetoric requires the ability to speak and write effectively.

- Understanding how one can use language to influence others is an important skill for democratic citizens.

- Democracy fundamentally depends on civil discourse among citizens.

- The ELA curriculum is a natural place to include discussions of rhetoric, writing, and speaking, and is where students can create and share their own writing.

Chapter 9

CIVICS LESSONS FOR SCIENCE AND MATHEMATICS

Although civics is typically specific to the domain of social studies and other humanities, there are countless opportunities for science and mathematics teachers to effectively incorporate civics into their lessons. This is particularly true when students engage with authentic, real-world tasks that involve various aspects of civic life.

In this chapter, we explore several original sample lessons for science and mathematics teachers, including those from both elementary and secondary levels. We also include a selection of high-quality lessons from reputable organizations that exemplify effective importation of civic learning in science and mathematics subject areas. For each lesson, we include the grade range, topics, standards connections, civics connections, time frame, lesson overview, and implementation steps, and a sample lesson in action to illustrate how it might play out in a classroom setting. Following each lesson is a list of go-to resources to help you implement and enrich each lesson. First, let's start by examining civics in the science class.

Civics in Science

At the writing of this book, the relationship between the scientific community and the public is precarious. This is mostly because science plays such a vital role in the development of public policy and its impact on society. For example, a 2020 Pew Research Center study asserts that "science issues, whether connected with climate, childhood vaccines, or new techniques in biotechnology, are part of the fabric of civic life, raising a range of social, ethical, and policy issues for the citizenry" (Funk, 2020). Although some of these debates around the validity of scientific claims fall along party lines (for example, climate change), not all of them do. For example, a relatively even number of vaccine skeptics identify as Democrats, Republicans, or Independent voters. One common thread is that the public's faith in the scientific community, particularly for issues that shape public policy, rises when the research and data are openly available to the public (Funk, 2020).

Elementary Science Lesson

In our first example, we provide a sample science lesson tailored for the elementary classroom. Along with an examination of science topics, such as weather and environmental impacts of human activity, students will explore the role of local government and community action to help mitigate weather-related challenges.

Community Solutions to Weather-Related Problems

- **Grade level:** 3
- **Topics:** Weather, environmental impact, design, cause and effect
- **Science standards connections:**
  - *3-ESS3-1*—Earth and Human Activity (Next Generation Science Standards [NGSS], n.d.b)
  - *Science 3 Content Standard*—Students are expected to know observable changes in the local environment caused by erosion and deposition by wind, water, and ice (British Columbia, n.d.e).
- **Civics connections:** Civics-related content, deliberation of issues, action civics
- **Time frame:** Two to three hours

Lesson Overview

In this lesson, students explore weather-related problems that impact their community. This exploration will preferably be tailored to the geographic location that they live in. Students then learn about and evaluate design solutions that reduce the negative impact of these weather-related challenges. In the last stage of the lesson, students research and deliberate around potential public policy solutions related to implementation of the mitigation strategies.

1. First, identify a weather-related challenge that faces your community. It could be a natural disaster–level challenge—such as hurricanes, tornadoes, wildfires—or it could be a more typical challenge such as extreme cold in the winter, excessive heat in the summer, or seacoast erosion. Once a challenge is identified, provide instruction and related resources to help students gain background knowledge of the weather-related event and its impact on the community.

2. Once students have a deeper understanding of the weather-related challenge and its impact on human activity, provide students with at least two design solutions that help prevent or at least reduce the negative impacts of these events. To extend the activity further, or provide enrichment opportunities, have students engage in their own research regarding possible mitigation strategies.

3. Now that students have been introduced to two or more solutions, have students evaluate each solution. More specifically, they should judge the merits of the solution based upon how well it meets the challenge presented by the weather-related event. Specific criteria can be developed to help scaffold the activity. As a class, engage in deliberation to narrow it down to one design solution chosen by the class as the preferred method.

4. At this point in the lesson, the class has chosen a preferred design solution to the weather-related challenge. Now, pose the first of two prompts.

    a. How can the local government help community members with this design solution? Depending on students' background knowledge, you may need to provide some specific examples to jumpstart the conversation. Have students individually, then collectively, brainstorm as many ways as possible.

    b. Should the local government require that all residents use the design solution? This question is a bit more complex, so again an example to provide context may be required. Another helpful strategy could be to categorize the positive consequences of mandating the solution, as well as the negative consequences.

5. As a lesson closure, start off a class discussion by asking students to list the stakeholders involved in the scenario that they just learned about. They should mention examples such as meteorologists, scientists, engineers, environmental advocates, community residents, and local government officials. A key takeaway to highlight for students is that an issue as complex as mitigating the negative impacts of weather-related challenges requires the collective expertise of many people and groups, along with their ability to effectively communicate and collaborate to solve the problem together.

Extension Activity

Consider having students design their own solution to the weather-related challenge. Students can then propose ideas related to how the local government can help promote or enact their design solution.

Sample Lesson in Action

To kick off a new science unit on weather, grade 3 teacher Mrs. Cohen asks students to brainstorm all the challenges people in their community face related to weather. Being a school in the northeastern United States, the three most common student responses include: *winter snowstorms*, *summer heat waves*, and *fall hurricanes*. Mrs. Cohen then asks students to rank the three challenges in order from most challenging (1) to least challenging (3). After a quick tally of the challenge that received the most rankings of 1—in this case, winter snowstorms—the class then moves into the research phase of the unit. Mrs. Cohen leads a minilesson that teaches students about hurricanes and their impact on local communities, while also curating a collection of related digital media that students can explore. She conducts a formative assessment to ensure student understanding before moving to the next phase—reteaching key content as needed.

Teacher Tip: Digital Tools for Visible Thinking and Brainstorming

When engaging students in brainstorming activities, consider using a digital tool or platform to facilitate the process. Popular tools include Google Forms (www.google.com/forms/about), Nearpod (https://nearpod.com), Jamboard (workspace.google.com/products/jamboard), and Padlet (https://padlet.com).

Mrs. Cohen then tasks students with designing solutions that can minimize the negative impacts snowstorms have on the community. Since the challenge is still very broad, Mrs. Cohen facilitates a group conversation in which students narrow down the specific snowstorm impact they would like to address, such as downed power lines and outages, leaving families without heat and, in some cases, running water. Now that they have identified a specific challenge, Mrs. Cohen provides groups with two design solutions. The first option is for communities to invest in underground power lines. The second option is to provide residents with more options for backup power via portable or fixed backup generators. Student groups then engage in an activity in which they evaluate the advantages and disadvantages of each option. Mrs. Cohen also provides groups with the option of researching an alternative option besides the two provided.

Following the initial discussion of advantages and disadvantages, Mrs. Cohen provides a graphic organizer specifying criteria that evaluate how well each option meets the challenges presented by winter storms. Once complete, the entire class engages in a discussion and selection protocol that identifies the design solution they feel best addresses the challenge.

The next phase of this experience includes the connection with, and role of, local government. Assuming that the class chooses the option of providing more options for backup power, Mrs. Cohen asks students how local government can assist with this solution. She provides an example, suggesting that local funding can be set aside for low-income families to offset the cost of purchasing a backup generator. After presenting several other examples, Mrs. Cohen asks if the local government should require that all residents have backup power, and then facilitates a class discussion around the benefits and drawbacks of that public policy approach.

Mrs. Cohen closes the lesson by discussing all the community members who might become involved in this scenario, such as meteorologists, scientists, environmental advocates, community residents, and local government officials. Mrs. Cohen also makes sure to discuss how complex these issues can be and how important it is for all types of community members to effectively work together to solve problems. To help create a more authentic, real-world connection, Mrs. Cohen invites a guest from the local town council to visit and hear students' suggestions and provide feedback to their design solution and its feasibility of implementation in the community.

Go-To Resources

Following are valuable resources to enrich this lesson and engage students.

- "Extreme Weather for Kids | Hurricanes, Tornadoes, Lightning | Science Lesson | Grades 3–5" (GenerationGenius, 2018)

- "Severe Weather: Crash Course Kids #28.2" (Crash Course Kids, 2015)
- "Winter Storms" (Northeast States Emergency Consortium, n.d.)
- "Counties Work" simulation (iCivics, n.d.b)

Secondary Science Lesson

The next sample science lesson is aimed at the secondary level. This lesson integrates the topics of ecology, population growth, and consumption, along with discussion of controversial issues, public policy, and advocacy.

Mitigating Human Impacts on Earth's Systems

- **Grade level:** 6–8
- **Topics:** Ecology, population growth, consumption
- **Science standards connections:**
  - *MS-ESS3-4*—Construct an argument supported by evidence for how increases in human population and per-capita consumption of natural resources impact Earth's systems (NGSS, n.d.d).
  - *Physical Geography*—Evaluate how particular geographic actions or events affect human practices or outcomes (geographical value judgments; British Columbia, n.d.d).
- **Civics connections:** Discussion of controversial issues, public policy, civic action and advocacy
- **Time frame:** About three hours

Lesson Overview

In this lesson, students explore evidence related to the various ways human population growth, particularly related to natural resource consumption, impacts the environment. Students explore various impacts, including composition and structure of Earth's systems, as well as the rate at which they change. Then, students evaluate several proposals designed to either reduce resource consumption, mitigate the negative impacts of consumption, or solutions that address both. The lesson concludes with students constructing written and oral arguments, supported by evidence and reasoning, advocating for a specific design solution.

1. Introduce the claim to students that increases in the size of the human population and increases in per-capita consumption of resources impact Earth's systems in various ways. Then provide resources and databases

students can research to evaluate the validity of that claim in various contexts. For example, they can evaluate graphs of the changes in population of regions over a specific length of time, then compare them to ecological changes during that same timespan in that ecosystem. Students also can explore ways that engineered solutions have changed the impact human activities have had on Earth's systems, for better or for worse.

2. Students narrow down the specific region, timespan, ecological impact, and engineered solution. They then evaluate evidence related to (1) human impact on that region's systems over the time period and (2) the effectiveness of the engineered solution. The key consideration is how sufficient the evidence is in determining the causal relationship between consumption and impact, as well as the causal relationship between the engineered solution and its ability to mitigate the negative environmental impact.

3. Students choose one of the engineered solutions and develop a public policy proposal. First, they research related public policy options in place and their effectiveness. After evaluating them, students craft a policy idea that encourages the engineered solutions, subsidizes the solutions, leads to further research of the solutions, mandates use of the solutions, or explores other related concepts.

Extension Activity

Students engage in outreach to local, state, or federal representatives and advocate for their chosen public policy proposal.

Sample Lesson in Action

Mr. Rollins starts off this lesson by displaying the following quote: "Human population growth and the resulting increase in natural resource consumption are making a significant impact on Earth's systems." He then instructs students to form small groups and discuss whether they believe the claim is true, and if so, what impacts on Earth's systems we are in fact experiencing.

After facilitating a large group debrief discussion, Mr. Rollins presents students with four resources to independently view and answer a series of comprehension questions about: (1) an interactive World Bank (n.d.) chart graphing population growth, (2) the Khan Academy (n.d.) video "Protecting Biodiversity: Local and Global Policies," (3) "Human Activities That Threaten Biodiversity" (PBS LearningMedia, n.d.), and (4) an interactive "BiomeViewer" in which students can explore "biomes, climate, biodiversity, and human impacts around the globe and at different times" (HHMI BioInteractive, n.d.a).

After students obtain more background knowledge on the role science plays in crafting public policy, they develop written and oral arguments advocating for their engineered solution. Mr. Rollins then encourages students to propose their solution to local, state, and federal officials, providing them with their official contact information and guidance on the most effective ways to engage in that communication.

> **Teacher Tip: Digital Station Rotations**
>
> For lessons that involve many different resources or learning modalities, consider using a rotational model. Set up a series of stations and leverage digital tools and content to enhance the student experience. You can create a teacher-led station or help facilitate students who need help as they navigate the different activities.

Go-To Resources

Following are valuable resources to enrich this lesson and engage students.

- Chart graphing population growth (World Bank, n.d.)
- "Protecting Biodiversity: Local and Global Policies" (Khan Academy, n.d.)
- "Human Activities That Threaten Biodiversity" (PBS LearningMedia, n.d.)
- "BiomeViewer" (HHMI BioInteractive, n.d.a)
- "The Anthropocene: Human Impact on the Environment" (HHMI BioInteractive, n.d.b)
- "Step Five: All About Public Policy" lesson from iCivics (n.d.f)

Civics in Mathematics

Although integrating civics into mathematics class may seem like a stretch, like science, there are many opportunities for the intersection between these important disciplines. As described by Professor Mary Candace Raygoza of Saint Mary's College of California:

> When we think about civics, we often think it's the social studies teacher's job. . . . But if we think about what it means to do mathematics as something we need for understanding and revealing what's going on in the

world—especially with pressing issues of social concern—we have to think about it as the job of the math teacher, too. (as cited in Sawchuk, 2019b)

In a research paper on the topic, Raygoza (2019) further explains a concept coined *quantitative civic literacy*:

As we do the work of reimagining mathematics classrooms as interdisciplinary, problem-posing spaces that connect to students' lives, communities, and the world, how can we help prepare young people to develop as civic actors, using their mathematical knowledge and skills to build their *quantitative civic literacy*? (p. 26)

In many ways, this research and the related scholarship on critical mathematics align closely with the action civics model discussed at several points earlier in this book. If your philosophy aligns with social justice education and similar approaches, mathematics can play a central role in these lessons and projects. If action civics and social justice education are not necessarily in your wheelhouse, there are countless other ways to incorporate civics into mathematics, such as analyzing electoral results, rates of taxation, national debts and deficits, public budgets, and much more. In the following section, we highlight lesson ideas that represent both the critical mathematics approach along with a more traditional intersection of civics and mathematics lessons.

Elementary Mathematics Lesson

The elementary mathematics lesson provides an elementary-level experience that focuses on data analysis and percentages. Throughout the lesson, we integrate civics concepts and themes such as elections, exit polling, and class deliberation.

Election Demographics

- **Grade level:** 5
- **Topics:** Data analysis, percentages, elections
- **Mathematics standards connections:**
  - *Mathematical Practice 3*—Construct viable arguments and critique the reasoning of others (NGA & CCSSO, 2010b).
  - *Mathematics 6 Content*—Whole-number percents and percentage discounts (British Columbia, n.d.b)
- **Civics connections:** Elections, exit polling, deliberation
- **Time frame:** About one hour

Lesson Overview

In this lesson, students analyze 2020 election data based on exit polling results. They also have the opportunity to break down the results by different demographics. After exploring specific cases and examples, students construct arguments based on different demographic groups that would have altered the election results. They then communicate their arguments and justifications with other students and evaluate the plausibility of each other's arguments.

1. Provide students with some background knowledge regarding what exit polling is and why organizations conduct it. Students may also need some additional background knowledge on elections in general, so a gauge of their understanding of the basic premise and function of presidential elections may be necessary before discussing the idea of exit polls.

2. Once students understand the context, pose several questions related to a set of exit poll data. Question types can vary, but make sure to address analysis of voting percentages and differences in percentages.

3. Students analyze a data set and design their own arguments. They identify a voting subgroup and determine what percentage increase would be needed for that candidate to achieve over 50 percent of the votes.

4. Once students develop their argument, they present it to the class. The class then has the opportunity to work out the problem to ensure the argument makes sense. If there's a flaw in the argument, the class can identify and explain it to the presenter.

5. Repeat the same process in step 4 for the remaining students, so each student has an opportunity to evaluate each other's argument and provide feedback.

Extension Activity

Students research and explore careers and other real-world situations in which people need to effectively evaluate election data and make informed decisions based on that information.

Sample Lesson in Action

Ms. Ogawa begins the lesson by asking students the following question: "What does mathematics have to do with presidential elections, if anything?" Ms. Ogawa asks students to enter their answers into a Google Form to collect and visually display their responses for a follow-up discussion. After debriefing on the opening prompt,

Ms. Ogawa recognizes that students have a difficult time making the connections and lack a basic understanding of elections. She also knows students will be examining exit poll data and surmises that she will need to teach them about exit polls.

To help build context, Ms. Ogawa engages students in the fifteen- to twenty-minute iCivics (n.d.a) simulation "Cast Your Vote," which teaches students the basics of participating in an election. She also creates a modified version of an article explaining exit polls provided by the American Association for Public Opinion Research (n.d.). This narrows down the information to the need-to-know facts for this lesson. She conducts a quick formative assessment to gauge student understanding of elections and exit polling, reteaching specific points as necessary.

> **Teacher Tip: Formative Assessment Practices**
>
> Giving quick formative assessments throughout a lesson provides students with timely and relevant feedback, helping them adjust their course. These assessments also provide key performance data that can help you adjust instruction when necessary. Consider leveraging digital tools to increase efficiency and provide rapid, even real-time results. Commonly used digital formative assessment tools include Google Forms (www.google.com/forms/about), Pear Deck (www.peardeck.com), Nearpod (https://nearpod.com), and Kahoot! (https://kahoot.com).

Ms. Ogawa presents students with a chart of 2020 presidential election exit poll data from *The New York Times* (n.d.). She places students into groups and assigns each group specific sets of mathematics problems based on the data set. For example, she asks one group the following: "Based on the exit poll data, what percentage of males voted for Donald Trump? What was the difference in percentages? Roughly 155 million U.S. citizens voted in the 2020 presidential election. Assuming the exit polls were accurate, how many more males in total voted for President Trump?"

Next, Ms. Ogawa challenges students to develop their own arguments based on the data. She instructs them to make a claim that reflects a change in a subgroup's voting percentage that would have significantly influenced the outcome. For example, if 52 percent of the 155 million voters were women, and only 42 percent voted for Donald Trump, how many more women in total would have needed to vote for Trump for him to reach 50 percent of all women's votes? Now that each group has a claim based on the exit poll data, group members present their claim to another group. The other group is instructed to evaluate the validity of the claim and provide feedback to the original group. Ms. Ogawa then instructs groups to switch roles so each group has the opportunity to evaluate each other's claim.

To close out this experience, Ms. Ogawa highlights several careers that specialize in knowing how to analyze and make use of election data, like the experience they just engaged in. Using the resource "So You Want to Work in Political Data" (Strasburger, 2020), the class discusses the different roles and opportunities in this line of work. Ms. Ogawa asks, "Even if it were not your profession, what other circumstances may arise in which you would need to know how to analyze election information? As a citizen? As a representative or candidate running for office? As a business?" She then concludes with an explanation that mathematics is an effective way to gain a deeper understanding about a variety of issues and help solve challenges across various domains, such as this lesson.

Go-To Resources

Following are valuable resources to enrich this lesson and engage students.

- "Cast Your Vote" election simulation (iCivics, n.d.a)
- "National Exit Polls: How Different Groups Voted" (*The New York Times*, n.d.)
- "Explaining Exit Polls" (American Association for Public Opinion Research, n.d.)
- "So You Want to Work in Political Data" (Strasburger, 2020)

Secondary Mathematics Lesson

The secondary mathematics lesson is aimed at the high school level and based on the theme of relationships between zip codes and life expectancy. The mathematics topics addressed include data analysis, graphing, probability, and statistics.

Zip Code and Life Expectancy

- **Grade range:** 9–12
- **Topics:** Data analysis, graphing, probability and statistics
- **Mathematics standards connections:**
  - *CCSS.Math-Content.S-IC.B.3*—Recognize the purposes of and differences among sample surveys, experiments, and observational studies (NGA & CCSSO, 2010b).
  - *Mathematical Practice 3*—Construct viable arguments and critique the reasoning of others (NGA & CCSSO, 2010b).

> *Mathematics 9 Content*—Statistics in society (British Columbia, n.d.c)

> *Statistics 12 Curriculum Competency*—Develop, demonstrate, and apply conceptual understanding of statistical ideas through play, story, inquiry, and research (British Columbia, n.d.g).

- **Civics connections:** Public policy, advocacy
- **Time frame:** About one hour

Lesson Overview

In this lesson, students analyze demographic data based on life expectancy and health care expenditures. They then create graphs using various data sets related to those core topics. Last, students develop arguments based on data and communicate these to others in the class.

1. Provide students with a variety of demographic data sets, charts, and graphs, along with problems to solve related to the data sets.

2. Give students open-ended prompts to encourage them to dive into the data sets to make arguments and draw conclusions. For example, "Is there a correlation between zip code, life expectancy, and health expenditures?"

3. Have students engage in research to find related data sets, charts, and graphs that can illuminate more about the complex issue being studied.

4. After students have researched a wider scope of data related to the issue, have them develop an argument backed up by the data. Students then present their arguments to the class and evaluate the validity of each other's claims.

Extension Activity

Have students engage in research around public policy related to health care and how analysis of data plays a vital role in policy development and implementation.

Sample Lesson in Action

Mr. Martinez starts with the following prompt: "How can mathematics, particularly statistics and data analysis, help both identify and solve problems in our society?" Mr. Martinez uses a presentation and visualization tool called Mentimeter to display responses and trends for the class to view and help spark ideas and enrich the discussion (see www.mentimeter.com). He then provides students with two resources—a Centers for Disease Control and Prevention (CDC) report on mortality rates in 2018

(Xu, Murphy, Kochanek, & Arias, 2020) and the article "Life Expectancy: Could Where You Live Influence How Long You Live?" (Robert Wood Johnson Foundation, n.d.). In small groups, students work through a series of problems designed by Mr. Martinez to help them comprehend and analyze the data in each resource.

Mr. Martinez debriefs with the class to ensure students are able to correctly interpret the data, and then provides them with a third resource, the article "What's Going on in This Graph? Global Life Expectancy & Health Expenditures: How Has the Relationship Between Life Expectancy and Health Expenditures by Country Changed Since 2000?" (The Learning Network, 2021). Mr. Martinez then offers the following prompts: "What do you notice? What do you wonder? What impact do you think this has on our own community?" The class then engages in a second follow-up discussion based on these prompts.

> **Teacher Tip: Digital Tools for Data Visualizations**
>
> When creating resources for students, consider using high-quality digital tools to graph and visualize data, such as Google Sheets (www.google.com/sheets/about), which provides several ready-made visualizations based on the existing data. You also can use a tool like Adobe Creative Cloud Express (www.adobe.com/express) or Canva for Education (www.canva.com/education) to create stunning infographics with their wide selection of templates and creation tools. Students also can use these tools when creating visualizations and graphics as part of class activities or projects.

Now that students have some background knowledge on the issue and experience analyzing data, Mr. Martinez asks them to take it a step further. Based on this complex issue, the correlation between location, mortality rates, and health care expenditures, students engage in research to find related studies, graphs, and data sets to help illuminate the issue. Mr. Martinez also encourages students to focus on their local region. Once complete, Mr. Martinez instructs students to present their key findings to each other in small groups.

As a lesson closure, Mr. Martinez leads a discussion about how data collection and analysis play such a vital role in public policy development and implementation, particularly with an issue as complex as public health and health care.

Go-To Resources

Following are valuable resources to enrich this lesson and engage students.

- Mentimeter presentation and polling tool (www.mentimeter.com)

- "Life Expectancy: Could Where You Live Influence How Long You Live?" (Robert Wood Johnson Foundation, n.d.)
- "Mortality in the United States, 2018" (Xu et al., 2020)
- "What's Going on in This Graph? Global Life Expectancy & Heath Expenditures: How Has the Relationship Between Life Expectancy and Health Expenditures by Country Changed Since 2000?" (The Learning Network, 2021)

Conclusion

The lesson examples in this chapter demonstrate how you can effectively integrate civics themes and skills into both science and mathematics courses at the elementary and secondary levels. These lessons are, of course, just a starting point and hopefully a spark of inspiration for teachers looking to authentically weave civics into their curriculum. Let your own creativity guide you in making authentic connections between your content area and real-world scenarios that both engage students and prepare them for modern citizenry.

Key Takeaways for Civics Lessons for Science and Mathematics

Following are key takeaways from this chapter on civics lessons for science and mathematics.

- Although civics is typically in the social studies domain, there are countless opportunities for science and mathematics teachers to effectively incorporate civics into their lessons.
- A key strategy is to pair elements of your mathematics or science curriculum with authentic, real-world tasks that involve various aspects of civic life.
  - A science example is pairing environmental science or ecology with public policy actions.
  - A mathematics example is pairing data analysis and visualizations with election results.

Chapter 10

INTERDISCIPLINARY CIVICS EXPERIENCES

Some of the most powerful learning experiences teachers can craft for students are interdisciplinary in nature. In this chapter, we explore practical examples of civics learning through this multi-subject approach. These examples are authentic, interdisciplinary lessons that include content and skills from the four major subject areas—ELA, mathematics, social studies, and science—tied to subject-specific standards.

Each experience is designed to apply the promising practices of effective civic education we have advocated throughout the book, such as deliberations on controversial topics, student voice, simulations of adult civic roles, news media literacy, and civic action. Like in chapters 7, 8, and 9, we also include a list of recommended resources for each that highlights go-to digital content and tools that can help amplify the impact of these lessons.

Elementary Interdisciplinary Civics Experience

We begin with an example of an interdisciplinary civics learning experience designed for the elementary classroom. The design incorporates the four core subject areas of mathematics, science, ELA, and social studies, and addresses specific subject and grade-level standards from each. You can implement these ideas in various ways over multiple lessons or days, but we advocate doing as much as possible to effectively weave the subjects together whenever possible.

For example, when students engage in a mathematics lesson in which they analyze emissions data, it is not just a stand-alone lesson. Instead, it is part of the larger experience, and you should communicate that to students. We understand that school structures and schedules are not always conducive to long blocks of interdisciplinary learning. However, you can still make connections for students to the bigger picture, even if the experience is structured in subject-specific blocks of time during the school day. The following experience also has students engage in deliberation of controversial issues, lateral reading strategies, and civic action.

Climate Science and Our School

- **Grade level:** 5
- **Topics:** Climate change, data analysis, public policy research, and persuasive writing
- **Content standards connections:**
  - *3-5-ETS1-1 Engineering Design*—Define a simple design problem reflecting a need or a want that includes specified criteria for success and constraints on materials, time, or cost (NGSS, n.d.a).
  - *Mathematical Practice 3*—Construct viable arguments and critique the reasoning of others (NGA & CCSSO, 2010b).
  - *CCSS.ELA-Literacy.W.5.1*—Write opinion pieces on topics or texts, supporting a point of view with reasons and information (NGA & CCSSO, 2010a).
  - *National Curriculum Standards for Social Studies*—Civic Ideals and Practices (NCSS, n.d.).
  - *Science 5*—Identify questions to answer or problems to solve through scientific inquiry (British Columbia, n.d.f).
  - *English Language Arts 5*—Create and communicate (writing, speaking, representing); exchange ideas and perspectives to build shared understanding (British Columbia, n.d.a).
- **Civics connections:** Deliberation of controversial issues, lateral reading strategies, civic action
- **Time frame:** Four to five hours

Lesson Overview

In the following interdisciplinary experience, students explore the science of climate change, analyze emissions data, research mitigation strategies, and design a plan for their school. Once they develop their plan, each student will write a persuasive essay advocating for their ideas and present it to local policy stakeholders.

1. **Driving question:** "How might our school community take steps to help reduce global warming?" Engage students in an initial brainstorming session and gauge their overall level of background knowledge of the topic. Explain to students that this driving question will guide them throughout the learning experience.

2. **Science focus:** Engage students in a minilesson on climate change. Provide various resources that help build background knowledge on the basics of what climate change is and what human behaviors factor into global warming.

3. **Mathematics focus:** With this background knowledge, students now take a deeper dive into how much Earth is warming over time as well as each nation's carbon emissions. Have students analyze data and make calculations. First, give them a graph of average global temperature over time, along with problems to solve based on the data. For example, use the article "Climate Change: Global Temperature" (2021) by Rebecca Lindsey and LuAnn Dahlman. Review any specific mathematics formulas or strategies, as needed, to help solve the problems.

   Next, provide students with a chart of carbon emissions by country and have them solve problems that involve analysis of those data. For example, you can use the article "Each Country's Share of CO2 Emissions" (2022) by the Union of Concerned Scientists. Review responses to this activity as well and gauge student comprehension and skill.

4. **Social studies focus:** Now that students have background knowledge of climate change and have taken a deeper dive into the data, have them explore various public policies aimed at mitigating the effects of climate change. Provide students with a resource that explains some of the key focus areas of the Paris Climate Accords and how different countries are attempting to reduce emissions (United Nations, 2022). One option is to provide materials related to climate policy advocacy, such as the 2019 student-led climate strike and the Greta Thunberg speech (visit https://youtu.be/KAJsdgTPJpU to watch this speech).

5. **ELA focus:** Now return to the design challenge: *How might our school community take steps to help reduce global warming?* Give students a resource that highlights steps that schools can take to help reduce emissions and other mitigation strategies; for example, "10 Ways to Reduce Carbon Footprint in Schools" (CO2nsensus, 2021). Students then engage in research, finding and analyzing at least three related online sources. Before they begin, provide initial guidance, particularly related to lateral reading and other news media literacy strategies.

   Place students in small groups to craft a list of three steps the school should take to help reduce their school's carbon emissions. Groups then deliberate and prepare to discuss their list with the whole class and defend their position on their three steps. Following the whole-class discussion, students can choose one action for which to advocate, even if it is an idea from another group. Then have students write a persuasive essay advocating for their solutions.

Extension Activity

Students can present their ideas with an oral presentation to the class or to a local stakeholder involved in decision making regarding the proposal presented in their persuasive essay. For example, they could present their idea to a school committee member or at a town council meeting. If the logistics of physical attendance are a barrier, students could use a video creation tool to archive and share their ideas digitally and asynchronously.

Sample Lesson in Action

Mrs. Kershaw, eager to begin a new interdisciplinary experience with students, announces that they will be designing some new ideas for their school community. She then projects the design challenge on the wall: *How might our school community take steps to help reduce global warming?* Students take a few moments to individually think through a response and then add their ideas to a Google Form posted by Mrs. Kershaw in the Google Classroom platform. As students finish up, she scans through the responses for emerging themes and realizes that many students are unsure of specific steps to take at the school level. She encourages them, stating that they will have opportunities to learn more about this topic before they finalize any proposed solutions.

Mrs. Kershaw then shows the class a brief introductory video, "Causes and Effects of Climate Change" (*National Geographic*, 2017), to kick things off. She follows up by having students read the article "Carbon Dioxide Levels Are at a Record High. Here's What You Need to Know" (Nunez, 2019). Students complete a list of comprehension questions to gauge their understanding of the video and article. Once Mrs. Kershaw feels confident in their background knowledge, she tells students that they will now explore the mathematics of climate science to gain a deeper understanding of the issue.

The mathematics-focused part of the experience starts with a graph of global temperature change over time. Mrs. Kershaw references the article "Climate Change: Global Temperature" (Lindsey & Dahlman, 2021) and asks questions such as, "What do the bars in the graph actually represent?" or "Which three years have the highest temperatures relative to the long-term average?"

The second data set Mrs. Kershaw presents to students includes total carbon dioxide (CO_2) emissions by country along with each country's population. She accesses these data via the International Energy Agency (n.d.) web resource, the "IEA Atlas of Energy." She then poses several problems for students to solve, such as, "After calculating the CO_2 emissions per capita for the nations included in the graph, which three had the highest percentage? Which three had the lowest?" Mrs. Kershaw then reviews the answers with students and provides reteaching, as necessary, for any common mistakes or misconceptions regarding the graph and data analysis.

Mrs. Kershaw then tells the class that with this greater knowledge of the issues, they will explore ways that countries are trying to address the challenge through public policy. To kick things off, students read the following article as a class: "What Is the Paris Climate Agreement and Why Did the U.S. Rejoin?" (Briggs, 2021). Since the article may be a difficult read for some of the students, Mrs. Kershaw helps explain advanced vocabulary and terminology as they review the article as a whole group. Mrs. Kershaw then leads a follow-up conversation related to actual steps countries have pledged to take to address climate change concerns. She then shifts students' focus to climate change advocacy.

Using the Newsela platform, Mrs. Kershaw assigns an article highlighting the advocacy work of Greta Thunberg and her 2019 United Nations speech (*Los Angeles Times*, 2019). A key feature of Newsela is one can adapt an article to reading levels ranging from grade 3 through grade 12, which enables all students to access the content at their level of comprehension. To provide more context, Mrs. Kershaw reviews the PBS NewsHour Extra article, "Youth-Led Climate Protests Connect Students Around the Globe" (Adu-Wadier, 2019). After a debrief discussion with the class, it's time for students to research and design solutions for their school.

> ### Teacher Tip: Close-Reading Strategies
> It is often helpful to model close-reading strategies for students, including highlighting key vocabulary terms, annotating the text using varying criteria,

> and asking questions in the margins. Digital tools, such as Google Docs and the Newsela annotation feature, can enhance students' ability to engage in close-reading strategies while also providing the teacher with more streamlined processes of gauging student performance and giving timely and targeted feedback.

Mrs. Kershaw signals the shift toward the ELA-focus part of the learning experience, announcing that each student will take their idea and craft a persuasive essay justifying the need for their proposal. She informs students that the audience for their proposal will be the local school committee. Students use Google Docs to craft their essays and share them with Mrs. Kershaw through Google Classroom. Mrs. Kershaw then offers students feedback in the document through the comment feature, along with live conferencing with students in class.

Once their individual essays are complete, students each create an *elevator pitch* of their proposal and record it into a class topic in the Flipgrid (info.flipgrid.com) platform. Mrs. Kershaw then assigns other students' pitches and asks them to provide feedback using the reply feature in Flipgrid. Students use this feedback to make any final revisions to their persuasive essays. As an extension activity, Mrs. Kershaw asks if any students would like to present their proposals live to a school committee member. For those who volunteer, Mrs. Kershaw sets up a time to meet with school committee members. As an alternative, students can send their Flipgrid pitch videos directly to the committee members for review, and hopefully, receive feedback from them within the platform.

Go-To Resources

Following are valuable resources to enrich this lesson and engage students.

- "Causes and Effects of Climate Change" (*National Geographic*, 2017)
- "Carbon Dioxide Levels Are at a Record High. Here's What You Need to Know" (Nunez, 2019)
- "Climate Change: Global Temperature" (Lindsey & Dahlman, 2021)
- IEA Atlas of Energy (IEA, n.d.)
- "What Is the Paris Climate Agreement and Why Did the US Rejoin?" (Briggs, 2021)
- "Young Activist Makes Strong Speech to U.N. About Climate Change" (*Los Angeles Times*, 2019)
- "Youth-Led Climate Protests Connect Students Around the Globe" (Adu-Wadier, 2019)

- "10 Ways to Reduce Carbon Footprint in Schools" (CO2nsensus, 2021)
- "Sort Fact From Fiction Online With Lateral Reading" video from the Stanford History Education Group (2020)
- Flipgrid (info.flipgrid.com)

Secondary Interdisciplinary Civics Experience

One challenging aspect of being an informed citizen is the ability to evaluate, break down, and understand complex issues. The following learning experience represents how a team of teachers can collaborate in tackling a controversial subject in a way that includes family and community and promotes civil discourse and listening to opposing views, while building student capacity to make informed choices.

The Policy, Politics, and Science of Vaccines

- **Grade range:** 10–12
- **Topics:** Vaccinations, pandemics, immune system, government policy, probability, narrative histories
- **Content standards connections:**
  - **ELA:**
    - *CCSS.ELA-Literacy.RL.9–10.1*—Cite strong and thorough textual evidence to support analysis of what the text says explicitly as well as inferences drawn from the text (NGA & CCSSO, 2010a).
    - *CCSS.ELA-Literacy.RL.11–12.1*—Cite strong and thorough textual evidence to support analysis of what the text says explicitly as well as inferences drawn from the text, including determining where the text leaves matters uncertain (NGA & CCSSO, 2010a).
    - *2.1 Drafting-Focus on Content*—Select and organize ideas and information to draft texts appropriate for the purpose and audience (Ontario Ministry of Education, 2007).
  - **Mathematics:**
    - *CCSS.Math-Content.S-CP.A.5*—Recognize and explain the concepts of conditional probability and independence in everyday language and everyday situations (NGA & CCSSO, 2010b).

› **Science:**
  - *HS-LS2-8*—Evaluate evidence for the role of group behavior on individual and species' chances to survive and reproduce (NGSS, n.d.c).

▸ **Civics connections:** Discern fact from fiction; make informed choices; sift through and evaluate information; understand science, mathematics, and history to examine government responses to COVID-19; weigh opinions; participate in civil discourse; understand the effects of policies on individuals.

▸ **Time frame:** About two hours per subject

Lesson Overview

One of the effective practices of civic education is deliberations of current and controversial topics. This interdisciplinary unit explores this relevant topic of utmost societal importance that is (at the time of this writing) very controversial. We advocate embracing the complexity of these topics. This unit will construct understanding within each subject area while also exploring the scientific, mathematical, and social implications as well as the roots of the controversy.

Structuring interdisciplinary experiences in the high school setting requires coordination, but you could teach this unit concurrently or sequentially in coordination among teachers across subject areas.

1. **Social studies strand (U.S. history, part 1):** Step 1 explores the history of pandemics in the United States and how the government and society reacted to them. Give students a common overview article (for example, "A Bibliography of Historians' Responses to COVID-19: Primary Sources and Teaching Tools" [n.d.a] by the American Historical Association), and then allow them to select one of the following topics based on their personal interest.

   › Polio in the 1950s
   › Smallpox in the United States since 1700
   › Cholera outbreak of 1832
   › The yellow fever epidemic of 1878
   › The American influenza epidemic of 1918–1919
   › The bird flu
   › Measles in the 20th century

Once students read the materials, have them join interest groups and explore a combination of materials provided by the teacher and those they research and locate themselves. Once they have completed their research, students engage in a whole-class dialogue examining the government role in addressing each epidemic to develop an overview of government responses.

Students then return to their groups to respond to share their initial reactions to the class discussion. Once completed, each student writes an editorial opinion article to share his or her position regarding the questions: "Under what conditions should people be required to be vaccinated? What consequence, if any, should exist if they do not?" Students can submit their assignments online, where classmates will review their work and respond with two positives of the work and an area for growth.

2. **Science strand:** In step 2, students explore the human immune response, how it works, and how a vaccine can strengthen the immune response. They then examine how vaccines are made, including the cost of developing them. Next, students simulate how diseases spread with and without vaccines and behavioral changes. Each student will experience both of the following simulations.

   > *Simulation 1 (www.learner.org/wp-content/interactive/envsci/disease /disease.html)*—This simulation asks students to identify and manipulate how disease spreads by adjusting population density and human interaction. Students also can adjust transmission rates.

   > *Simulation 2 (www.learner.org/wp-content/interactive/envsci /disease/disease.html?initLesson=1)*—This simulation is similar to simulation 1, but it includes the ability to adjust the vaccination rate of the population.

   Students examine how the effects of diseases vary depending on the length of the illness, the transmission rate, and vaccination percentage. Once they are finished with the simulation, students explore medical and scientific responses both past and present (article 1) to evaluate their effectiveness based on what they learned from the simulation. As a final assessment, students examine an historical example (article 2) and offer suggestions for how the response to the epidemic or pandemic could have been more effective based on what they learned in the unit.

> *Article 1*—"Medical and Scientific Responses: Past Pandemics and Epidemics" (American Historical Association, n.d.c)
> *Article 2*—"Medical and Scientific Responses: COVID-19" (American Historical Association, n.d.b)

3. **Mathematics strand:** Following the science portion of this experience, mathematics classes can explore the concept of probability in order to determine vaccine effectiveness rates. What does it mean for a vaccine to be 95 percent effective? You can examine this in two ways. First, explore what a 95 percent effective rate means by applying it to national, state, and local populations. Then examine what percentage of the population needs to be vaccinated to begin reducing the number of new cases. Finally, look at polling data to determine if enough of the population is willing to receive a vaccination to effect a change.

4. **ELA strand:** Narrative histories are a powerful form of storytelling. Ask students to explore narrative collections through StoryCorps (https://storycorps.org/stories). Once they have finished, students select two of their favorite narratives and reexamine and evaluate them using the Oral History Association's Best Practices (www.oralhistory.org/best-practices). Guide the class in a discussion to reflect on the chosen narratives and identify the strengths as well as the possible weaknesses. Have students take another look at their selected narratives and try to identify examples in which the narrator might be unreliable or ineffective.

   Once complete, explain to students that they will collect a modern narrative of the COVID-19 era using the online article "How to Gather the Oral Histories of COVID-19" (Levine, 2020). Students will interview someone about their personal experiences with COVID-19, the lockdown resulting from it, or some other aspect of what it was like to live through it. Students can create their own interview script, but they are required to include a question asking their interviewee about how the government's actions directly affected their life. Once completed, ask students to share their narratives with the class, and then display them in the school library. Students can select any of the many organizations listed in the article, collecting narratives of the era so their work becomes an official part of history (Cauvin, 2020).

5. **Social studies strand (U.S. history, part 2):** This final part of the experience asks students to revisit the question "Under what conditions should the government require vaccination? What, if anything, should be done if people refuse?" Have them watch the online video

"Influencing Public Policy: Vaccines" to explore how vaccines have influenced public policy (Retro Report, n.d.).

Ask students to then explore the origin of the anti-vaccination movement with the article, "A Discredited Vaccine Study's Continuing Impact on Public Health" (Haberman, 2015). After a brief class discussion, ask students to participate in a whole-class debate on the issue. Provide a possible government policy or a scenario on which students can share their opinions and responses based on their knowledge and understanding from this experience.

Sample Lesson in Action

Mr. Driver had been encouraging his team to work together to address a real-world issue that mattered to their students, and he was excited to find that they were eager to take on the task. Team members agreed to poll their classes to determine a topic for their interdisciplinary experience. The top two topics were (1) political and social division in the United States and (2) understanding the causes of the COVID-19 pandemic crisis. Rather than select only one of these topics, team members decided they could combine the two. Students were excited to hear the results of the poll, and that teachers were planning something new and exciting based on their feedback. More important than passing a test, the team hoped that they could create important dialogue, provide students with learning choices, and include opportunities for students to find their voices and express their opinions.

The team agreed to focus on the roles of the individual citizen and the government and to include dialogue, choice, and student expression into each of their lessons. Team members agreed that the culminating activity would be a structured debate in which students would call on the knowledge they gained. The team decided the debate would be a public event and invited teachers and local leaders. Members discussed how their subject areas could add to the experience. They shared their learning standards and started looking at the calendar. Once they agreed on a date, the plan started coming together.

They used their collaborative team time to share their lesson ideas with each other and started looking for ways to connect concepts and add to the big-picture understanding of the topic. The team was happy when the project started to become one big lesson plan dependent on each subject rather than several different lesson plans on the same topic.

Mr. Driver kicked off the lessons on Monday by setting up a conversation about government mask requirements. "When is it okay for the government to require someone to do something? When is it not okay?" After a while, he asked, "Should the government keep people safe?" and then followed up by asking, "Should the government require people to do something in the name of keeping people safe?" The hook was set.

Students dove into his lesson on the history of pandemics and epidemics in the United States. On Tuesday, the other teachers began their lesson. In the halls, it seemed everyone was discussing the topic. It was powerful for the team to see the buzz that its coordinated effort received. As the week proceeded, team members started to see the synergy of their combined efforts.

Mrs. Wrobel's science lesson on immunology was a hit. As she explained how vaccines were made, students were amazed to find out about how expensive the process could be and how hard it could be to prove that the vaccine was safe enough to receive government approval. The lesson emphasized that if enough people got vaccinated, diseases could be stopped without having to treat everyone.

In Ms. Gordon's mathematics class, students examined what a vaccine's effectiveness meant in terms of their city, their state, and for the whole country. They also enjoyed Mr. Thomas-Greene's activity in their English classes. Students explored the narrative writing process by interviewing a family member and then contributing their assignment to a narrative history project of their choice. Students were excited to choose which narrative history project to contribute to, such as the following.

- Princeton University's "Covid-19 & Me: Oral History Project" (https://bit.ly/3qPq3NI)
- HISTORY NOW: The Pandemic Diaries Project (www.nypl.org/pandemic-diaries)
- StoryCorps Connect (https://storycorps.org/participate/storycorps-connect)
- A Journal of the Plague Year—Oral History Project (https://covid-19archive.org/s/oralhistory/page/welcome)

By the time Mr. Driver began preparing for the culminating debate, students sounded like experts. When other teams saw the buzz created by the event and how energized the students had become, they wanted to know more about the project and how the team accomplished it. Mr. Driver was proud of his team and his students, but what made him the happiest was that the kids had used so much of what they learned in mathematics, science, and English to answer the question of what the role of government should be.

Go-To Resources

Following are valuable resources to enrich this lesson and engage students.

- "A Vaccine, or a Spike in Deaths: How America Can Build Herd Immunity to the Coronavirus" (Stevens, 2020)
- "What Does 95% Effective Mean? Teaching the Math of Vaccine Efficacy" (Young-Saver, 2021)
- The Habitable Planet, Unit 16: Disease Lab (University of Wisconsin–Stout, 2020)
- "2 Companies Say Their Vaccines Are 95% Effective. What Does That Mean?" (Zimmer, 2020)

Conclusion

The lessons in this chapter demonstrate how teachers can design and implement authentic interdisciplinary experiences grounded in best practices for civic education. They also demonstrate how the thoughtful and effective integration of instructional technologies can amplify the impact of effective teaching strategies. If crafting similar experiences in your own teaching context is feasible, we encourage you to run with these ideas! If you envision significant structural or cultural challenges to designing and implementing interdisciplinary lessons and projects, start small and keep things practical. Even a slight shift in your lesson design can lead to a positive impact on student learning in your classroom.

Key Takeaways for Interdisciplinary Civics Experiences

Following are key takeaways from this chapter on interdisciplinary civics experiences.

- Some of the most powerful learning experiences teachers can craft for students are interdisciplinary in nature.
- When designing interdisciplinary lessons, consider integrating promising practices of effective civic education, such as deliberations on controversial topics, simulations of adult civic roles, news media literacy, and civic action.
- Effective integration of digital tools and resources amplifies the impact of interdisciplinary experiences.

EPILOGUE

Well-prepared citizens need practice, and the best way to provide that practice is to give students a chance to participate and *be* citizens. How prepared are citizens if we never give them a chance to act in the role of citizen before we call on them to participate in a democracy?

Civic education needs to be transformed into something more like a driver's education course in which students can get behind the metaphorical wheel and practice the skills and decision making that keep them and others around them safe. Much like we don't want a car to veer off course, we don't want democracy to veer off course, either.

Past patterns of civics instruction are deeply ingrained into our habits, and changing them will require commitment, especially when it comes to granting students the freedom to take on authentic, real-world issues. These experiences are essential to building the skills students need in the future and in forming their individual identities as citizens.

As any parent knows, the hardest part of teaching a child to walk, swim, or ride a bike is the moment when we must decide if the time is right to let go and let them do it alone. It's euphoric to watch them thrive. The world is at a crossroads. We need to make sure that what students experience on the way to becoming citizens is meaningful so when the time comes for us to let go of the reins of democracy, they are confident and prepared to take them.

Following are key considerations for the future of civic education. We hope they will help guide you in creating a plan that meets the needs of your students and communities.

1. **The best way to prepare citizens is to have them actively participate and engage in democratic processes:** Despite this, civic education programs have not been well funded or prioritized. As a result, citizen education programs have been in decline in schools. The contentious political climate has led states to examine how to reform these programs to better prepare students for active participation in a democratic society. Schools are heroically positioned to address this need, and the research on how to do it is definitive (Levine & Kawashima-Ginsberg, 2017).

2. **Effective civics instruction increasingly focuses on skills, dispositions, and capacities:** Traditional approaches to teaching civics focused primarily on civic knowledge and a basic understanding of government structures and processes. Although this foundational knowledge is important, educators need different strategies to ensure students are not only informed, but also capable of being active and engaged in civic life. Research points to a collection of promising practices to achieve this goal, including deliberation of controversial issues, simulations of adult civic roles, student voice in schools, news media literacy, and action civics (Levine & Kawashima-Ginsberg, 2017).

3. **Action civics leads to real-world learning and student empowerment:** Grounded in experiential learning and collective action, action civics projects provide students with a practical way to apply their growing knowledge of societal challenges and civic institutions. This approach also encourages students to view institutions as entities that they can improve and change, bringing us closer to realizing founding ideals. Although variations exist, most action civics projects encourage students to identify and research societal issues, design public policy solutions to address them, and mobilize support for their public policy solutions.

4. **Civil discourse is a highly effective way to teach democratic values:** Students can observe civil discourse by participating in local government to address issues relevant to their lives. Participating in debate and dialogue teaches students how to construct their own arguments and analyze the arguments of others. Having students explore controversial topics can teach necessary norms, behaviors, and skills to engage in challenging situations. Engaging in these topics is key to teaching how to solve differences with others peacefully and respectfully.

5. **News media literacy is essential to combating the growing threat of fake news and disinformation:** The increasing proliferation of fake, misleading, and biased information and news coverage is one of the core challenges facing democracy. Educators play a vital role in helping students develop the skills needed to discover and evaluate online information, and high-quality news media literacy programs are available to support them. Online research and fact-checking tools can help students navigate the complex and ever-changing world of digital news media.

6. **Games and competitions have the power to enhance student engagement and deepen civic understanding:** Games such as those developed by iCivics immerse students in virtual experiences that simulate adult civic roles, such as voting, campaigning, advocating for policies, and defending civil liberties. Other tools, like gamified assessment platforms, provide teachers with even more versatility in leveraging the motivational power of games in their everyday lessons. Competitions and student showcases, such as the We the People Mock Congressional Hearings, Generation Citizen Civics Day, and Kidizenship contests, also provide students with opportunities to collaborate and share ideas with a wider audience through engaging, real-world experiences.

7. **Quality civic education is an equity issue. Interdisciplinary experiences create authenticity and ensure that civics instruction is equitable:** As demonstrated in chapters 7–10, there are many effective ways to incorporate civics across grade levels and content areas. Doing so typically results in more authentic, real-world tasks for students that ground content knowledge from other subject areas, such as mathematics or science, in an actual challenge facing communities. Since many schools simply do not designate enough blocks of time to focus on civics instruction, weaving it into other subject areas is ever more vital to ensure that all students have access to high-quality civic education.

A Call to Action for Teachers

Teachers are at the front line of high-quality civics instruction. For those who teach social studies, consider implementing the promising practices outlined in this book along with the educational technologies that can amplify the impact of your best lessons. For those who teach other subjects, or elementary teachers who have difficulty designating time for social studies, do your best to weave civics instruction into your other subject areas through authentic, interdisciplinary projects. For all teachers reading this book, we also ask that you advocate for support. Whether it is curriculum design, professional development, or teaching materials, we know this is difficult work, and the more support you have from your school, the higher quality experiences you will be able to provide your students. We know that these efforts require time, and that is not always easy to come by. Ultimately, you know your values by what you do and do not make time for. Investing in citizens and a healthy democracy will pay off when students are the caretakers of democracy.

A Call to Action for School and District Leaders

We understand the competing interests and constraints that school and district leaders grapple with daily. With that backdrop, we first ask you to evaluate where you think your learning community is on the spectrum of high-quality civics instruction. You may realize that there are already amazing things happening, so a first step is to acknowledge and share inspiring civics experiences that are underway. The next step is to consider what gaps remain.

- Do you clearly integrate civics into your curriculum across K–12 and subject areas?
- Do you allow teachers to discuss best practices and share tips for embedding experiences with their peers?
- Do you provide elementary teachers the time and space to teach civics?
- Do you provide materials, such as books and software subscriptions, to enhance civics instruction?
- Do you design and implement high-quality professional learning experiences to staff around best practices?

These are all questions that can help you narrow your focus, time, and resources to establish the best path forward toward effective civics instructions for students in your school community.

A Call to Action for Policymakers

There is growing momentum across the United States and Canada to enhance civics instruction. Various states in the United States are adopting new civic education guidance, and national legislation has garnered support through the Civics

Secures Democracy Act (S.879—Civics Secures Democracy Act; Congress.gov, n.d.). Regarding the Canadian education system, a 2019 report directly "calls on Canada and the provinces to take a more coordinated and sustained approach to building civic literacy across generations" (People for Education, 2019). Whether you are a local school board member or national representative, you have a vital role to play in the future of civic education. We ask that you support guidance and legislation that advocate for high-quality civic education for students. Mandates alone may only lead to frustration during implementation, so we also ask that you advocate for the resources and support needed to design and enhance civics instruction, particularly for those communities that do not have much of a foundation from which to start building.

A Call to Action for Parents

We are educators, but like many of you reading this book, we are also parents. Although this book is designed for the education community, most of the resources we share can be used by families to help reinforce a quality civic education on the home front. Tom's second and fourth graders often have questions about issues they hear about in media, from teachers, or even from friends. This includes everything from the Black Lives Matter movement to the impacts of climate change on his home state. Engaging students in discussions about current issues, sharing civics games and simulations, showing how to fact-check media—all these small steps can play a big difference in students' lives. So, for the parents out there, our simple call to action is to engage with your children in whatever way is most comfortable for you.

Conclusion

Preparing students to become informed, engaged, and productive members of democratic society is one of the most fundamental goals of the education system. We face modern challenges that make participating in civic life much different than in years past. Our goal for this book is to lay out a series of best practices that are both foundational in quality civics instruction while also leveraging new strategies and emerging technology resources that help address the shifting nature of what it means to be a modern citizen. To do this, civics instruction must become an active and engaging process that focuses on and allows students to use skills that they need throughout their lives. Citizenship is more than voting, and students can act as citizens well before they can vote.

Any steps you can take in your classes and your curriculum to enhance students' learning experiences can make a tremendous impact on their trajectory. Collectively, improvement in civics instruction will ultimately strengthen the health of democratic societies and their institutions. The work is difficult and humbling, but well worth it.

REFERENCES AND RESOURCES

Ackerman, R., Neale, I., & CfBT Education Trust. (2011). *Debating the evidence: An international review of current situation and perceptions.* Accessed at https://debate.uvm.edu/dcpdf/ESU_Report_debatingtheevidence_FINAL.pdf on January 27, 2022.

Abrams, Z. (2021, March). *Controlling the spread of misinformation.* Accessed at www.apa.org/monitor/2021/03/controlling-misinformation on January 11, 2022.

Adams, K. (2019, November 6). *What federal funding for civics reveals about American political discourse.* Accessed at www.marketplace.org/2019/11/06/what-federal-funding-for-civics-reveals-about-american-political-discourse on October 13, 2021.

Adu-Wadier, B. (2019, April 4). *Youth-led climate protests connect students around the globe.* Accessed at www.pbs.org/newshour/extra/2019/04/youth-led-climate-protests-connect-students-around-the-globe on April 30, 2021.

AllSides. (2021, March 7). *Biden signs executive order aimed at promoting voting rights.* Accessed at www.allsides.com/story/biden-signs-executive-order-aimed-promoting-voting-rights on March 9, 2021.

Alterea. (n.d.). *Agents of influence.* Accessed at www.altereainc.com/about-9 on October 7, 2021.

American Association for Public Opinion Research. (n.d.). *Explaining exit polls.* Accessed at www.aapor.org/Education-Resources/Election-Polling-Resources/Explaining-Exit-Polls.aspx on April 17, 2021.

American Historical Association. (n.d.a). *A bibliography of historians' responses to COVID-19: Primary sources and teaching tools.* Accessed at www.historians.org/news-and-advocacy/everything-has-a-history/a-bibliography-of-historians-responses-to-covid-19/primary-sources-and-teaching-tools on March 30, 2022.

American Historical Association. (n.d.b). *Medical and scientific responses: COVID-19.* Accessed at www.historians.org/news-and-advocacy/everything-has-a-history/a-bibliography-of-historians-responses-to-covid-19/medical-and-scientific-responses/medical-and-scientific-responses-covid-19 on October 15, 2021.

American Historical Association. (n.d.c). *Medical and scientific responses: Past pandemics and epidemics.* Accessed at www.historians.org/news-and-advocacy/everything-has-a-history/a-bibliography-of-historians-responses-to-covid-19/medical-and-scientific-responses/medical-and-scientific-responses-past-pandemics-and-epidemics on October 15, 2021.

American University. (n.d.). *The game studio*. Accessed at www.american.edu/gamelab/studio.cfm on March 24, 2021.

Anderson, J., & Rainie, L. (2021, November). *The future of digital spaces and their role in democracy*. Accessed at www.pewresearch.org/internet/2021/11/22/the-future-of-digital-spaces-and-their-role-in-democracy on January 11, 2022.

Annenberg Classroom. (n.d.). *Civic education*. Accessed at www.annenbergclassroom.org/glossary_term/civic-education on January 5, 2022.

Annenberg Public Policy Center. (2021). *Annenberg civics knowledge survey*. Accessed at www.annenbergpublicpolicycenter.org/political-communication/civics-knowledge-survey on January 11, 2022.

Apple App Store. (n.d.). *Informable*. Accessed at https://apps.apple.com/us/app/informable/id1486205705 on October 11, 2021.

Atwell, M., Bridgeland, J., & Levine, P. (2017). *Civic deserts: America's civic health challenge*. Accessed at www.ncoc.org/wp-content/uploads/2017/10/2017CHIUpdate-FINAL-small.pdf on February 2, 2022.

Ballard, P. J., Cohen, A. K., & Littenberg-Tobias, J. (2016). Action civics for promoting civic development: Main effects of program participation and differences by project characteristics. *American Journal of Community Psychology, 58*(3–4), 377–390.

Bandy, J. (2011). *What is service learning or community engagement?* Nashville, TN: Vanderbilt University Center for Teaching. Accessed at https://cft.vanderbilt.edu/guides-sub-pages/teaching-through-community-engagement on January 5, 2022.

Bennett, J. (2020, July 3). These teen girls are fighting for a more just future. *The New York Times*. Accessed at www.nytimes.com/2020/06/26/style/teen-girls-black-lives-matter-activism.html on February 6, 2021.

Biello, P., & Cohen, R. (2019, March). *N.H. students bring red-tailed hawk bill back to state house*. Accessed at www.nhpr.org/post/nh-students-bring-red-tailed-hawk-bill-back-state-house#stream/0 on January 12, 2022.

Briggs, H. (2021, April 22). *What is the Paris climate agreement and why did the US rejoin?* Accessed at www.bbc.com/news/science-environment-35073297 on April 30, 2021.

British Columbia. (n.d.a). *BC's curriculum: English language arts 5*. Accessed at https://curriculum.gov.bc.ca/curriculum/english-language-arts/5/core on January 13, 2022.

British Columbia. (n.d.b). *BC's curriculum: Mathematics 6*. Accessed at https://curriculum.gov.bc.ca/curriculum/mathematics/6/core on January 12, 2022.

British Columbia. (n.d.c). *BC's curriculum: Mathematics 9*. Accessed at https://curriculum.gov.bc.ca/curriculum/mathematics/9/core on January 13, 2022.

British Columbia. (n.d.d). *BC's curriculum: Physical geography*. Accessed at https://curriculum.gov.bc.ca/curriculum/social-studies/12/physical-geography on January 12, 2022.

British Columbia. (n.d.e). *BC's curriculum: Science 3*. Accessed at https://curriculum.gov.bc.ca/curriculum/science/3/core on January 12, 2022.

British Columbia. (n.d.f). *BC's curriculum: Science 5*. Accessed at https://curriculum.gov.bc.ca/curriculum/science/5/core on January 13, 2022.

British Columbia. (n.d.g). *BC's curriculum: Statistics 12*. Accessed at https://curriculum.gov.bc.ca/curriculum/mathematics/12/statistics on January 13, 2022.

Cambridge Dictionary. (n.d.). *Adjectives: Order*. Accessed at https://dictionary.cambridge.org/us/grammar/british-grammar/adjectives-order on January 11, 2022.

Carnegie Corporation of New York, & Center for Information and Research on Civic Learning and Engagement. (2003). *The civic mission of schools*. New York: Authors. Accessed at https://media.carnegie.org/filer_public/9d/0a/9d0af9f4-06af-4cc6-ae7d-71a2ae2b93d7/ccny_report_2003_civicmission.pdf on January 15, 2021.

Carney, E. N. (2020, February 24). *Educators push for more diverse voices in the young and energized electorate*. Accessed at https://thefulcrum.us/civic-education-2645214593 on February 6, 2021.

Cauvin, T. (2020, April 24). *Mapping public history projects about COVID 19*. Accessed at https://ifph.hypotheses.org/3225 on October 15, 2021.

CBS News. (2021, January 19). *Most Americans don't know what's in the Constitution: A crisis of civic education*. Accessed at www.cbsnews.com/news/constitution-americans-civics-test on January 11, 2022.

Center for Civic Education. (n.d.a). *High school*. Accessed at https://civiced.org/we-the-people/hearings/high-school on March 25, 2021.

Center for Civic Education. (n.d.b). *Program description*. Accessed at www.civiced.org/we-the-people/program-description on March 25, 2021.

Center for Civic Education. (n.d.c). *We the People overview*. Accessed at www.civiced.org/pdfs/WethePeopleOverview.pdf on March 25, 2021.

Center for Civic Education. (n.d.d). *What is Project Citizen?* Accessed at www.civiced.org/project-citizen on February 6, 2021.

Center for Information and Research on Civic Learning and Engagement. (2018, October 15). *So much for "slacktivism": Youth translate online engagement to offline political action*. Accessed at https://circle.tufts.edu/latest-research/so-much-slacktivism-youth-translate-online-engagement-offline-political-action on February 6, 2021.

Centers for Disease Control and Prevention. (2021, June 16). *Drowning prevention*. Accessed at www.cdc.gov/drowning/prevention/index.html on January 6, 2022.

Checkology. (n.d.a). *Understanding bias*. Accessed at https://get.checkology.org/lesson/understanding-bias on February 22, 2021.

Checkology. (n.d.b). *What is Checkology?* Accessed at https://get.checkology.org/what-is-checkology on February 22, 2021.

Citizen Math. (n.d.). *You're so fined*. Accessed at www.mathalicious.com/lessons/you-re-so-fined on April 15, 2021.

Civic Action Project. (2019a, February 24). *Examples of civic action projects*. Accessed at https://crfcap.org/mod/page/view.php?id=231#filter-tabs-content-1-1 on February 7, 2021.

Civic Action Project. (2019b, April 19). *Wolf Lake BGCCF After School Zone Civic Education Marketing Synopsis*. Accessed at https://drive.google.com/file/d/1zdcJyVqeV7h_IBJmcYKyzQBhdM50xHvP/view on January 13, 2021.

Civic Online Reasoning. (n.d.a). *About*. Accessed at https://cor.stanford.edu/about on February 22, 2021.

Civic Online Reasoning. (n.d.b). *Evaluating evidence about climate change*. Accessed at https://cor.stanford.edu/curriculum/lessons/evaluating-evidence-science on April 20, 2021.

Civic Online Reasoning. (n.d.c). *Lateral reading about renewable energy*. Accessed at https://cor.stanford.edu/curriculum/lessons/lateral-reading-science on April 22, 2021.

Civic Online Reasoning. (n.d.d). *Lateral reading vs. vertical reading*. Accessed at https://cor.stanford.edu/curriculum/lessons/lateral-vs-vertical-reading on February 22, 2021.

Civic Online Reasoning. (n.d.e). *Teaching lateral reading*. Accessed at https://cor.stanford.edu/curriculum/collections/teaching-lateral-reading on February 22, 2021.

Claffey, J. (2015, March 20). *NH fourth graders' bill on state bird sends lawmakers on bizarre abortion rant.* Accessed at https://patch.com/new-hampshire/nashua/nh-lawmakers-destroy-fourth-graders-bill-liken-it-abortion-claim-it-wastes-ti-0 on January 5, 2022.

CO2nsensus. (2021, June 29). *10 ways to reduce carbon footprint in schools* [Blog post]. Accessed at www.co2nsensus.com/blog/reducing-carbon-footprint-in-schools on April 30, 2021.

Cohen, C., Kahne, J., Marshall, J., Anderson, V., Brower, M., & Knight, D. (2018). *Let's go there: Making a case for race, ethnicity and a lived civics approach to civic education.* Accessed at www.civicsurvey.org/publications/lets-go-there on January 11, 2022.

Collaborative for Academic, Social, and Emotional Learning. (2021, November 11). *School districts nationwide share insights for sustaining social and emotional learning.* Accessed at https://casel.org/school-districts-nationwide-share-insights-for-sustaining-social-and-emotional-learning-sel on December 31, 2021.

Collaborative for Academic, Social, and Emotional Learning. (2022a). *SEL and civic learning.* Accessed at https://casel.org/fundamentals-of-sel/how-does-sel-support-your-priorities/sel-and-civic-learning on January 5, 2022.

Collaborative for Academic, Social, and Emotional Learning. (2022b). *What is the CASEL framework?* Accessed at https://casel.org/fundamentals-of-sel/what-is-the-casel-framework/ on January 5, 2022.

Common Sense Education. (n.d.). *Digital citizenship curriculum.* Accessed at www.commonsense.org/education/digital-citizenship/curriculum?topic=news--media-literacy on February 22, 2021.

Common Sense Education. (2018). *Topic: News and media literacy.* Accessed at www.commonsense.org/education/digital-citizenship/topic/news-and-media-literacy on February 22, 2021.

Common Sense Media. (n.d.). *What should I teach my kid about safe online behavior?* Accessed at www.commonsensemedia.org/cyberbullying/what-should-i-teach-my-kid-about-safe-online-behavior on October 7, 2021.

Congress.gov. (n.d.). *S.879—Civics Secures Democracy Act.* Accessed at www.congress.gov/bill/117th-congress/senate-bill/879 on May 8, 2021.

Constitutional Rights Foundation. (2017, March 22). *Inglewood gentrification—Civic action project* [Video file]. Accessed at https://youtu.be/hantezGIwRQ on February 7, 2021.

Constitutional Rights Foundation. (2018). *Educating about immigration: DREAM Act.* Accessed at http://crfimmigrationed.org/proposed-legislation/dream-act on December 20, 2021.

Crash Course. (2019, March 5). *Click restraint: Crash course navigating digital information #9* [Video file]. Accessed at https://youtu.be/5tw44SkkXQg on March 5, 2021.

Crash Course. (2020, August 20). *Navigating digital information* [Video playlist]. Accessed at https://youtube.com/playlist?list=PL8dPuuaLjXtN07XYqqWSKpPrtNDiCHTzU on March 5, 2021.

Crash Course Kids. (2015, September 25). *Severe weather: Crash course kids #28.2* [Video file]. Accessed at www.youtube.com/watch?v=QVZExLO0MWA on April 19, 2021.

Democratic Knowledge Project. (n.d.). *Our work.* Accessed at www.democraticknowledgeproject.org/about-us/work on January 14, 2021.

Denny, S. A., Quan, L., Gilchrist, J., McCallin, T., Shenoi, R., Yusuf, S., et al. (2019). Prevention of drowning. *American Academy of Pediatrics, 143*(5), e20190850. Accessed at https://doi.org/10.1542/peds.2019-0850 on January 11, 2022.

Desilver, D. (2018, June 18). *Q&A: Telling the difference between factual and opinion statements in the news.* Accessed at www.pewresearch.org/fact-tank/2018/06/18/qa-telling-the-difference-between-factual-and-opinion-statements-in-the-news on January 11, 2022.

Driscoll, T., & McCusker, S. (2020). Innovation in civic education: Preparing citizens for a modern world. In L. Kyei-Blankson, E. Ntuli, & M. Nur-Awaleh (Eds.), *Emerging techniques and applications for blended learning in K–20 classrooms* (pp. 186–203). Hershey, PA: IGI Global.

d.school Institute of Design at Stanford. (n.d.). *An introduction to design thinking: Facilitator's guide—Script, talking points, takeaways, and setup considerations inside.* Accessed at https://dschool.stanford.edu/s/Facilitators-Guide_Design-Thinking.pdf on January 14, 2022.

Duer, C. (2016). *The civic education crisis and its effect on young voters.* Accessed on https://trace.tennessee.edu/utk_bakerschol/36 on January 18, 2021.

Edwards, J., & Smolinski, R. (Ed.). (1741). Sinners in the hands of an angry God. A sermon preached at Enfield, July 8th, 1741. *Electronic Texts in American Studies, 54.* Accessed at https://digitalcommons.unl.edu/etas/54 on March 5, 2020.

Earth Force. (n.d.). *Earth Force process.* Accessed at https://earthforceresources.org/efprocess on October 8, 2021.

Earth Force. (2013). *A curriculum for community action and problem solving.* Accessed at http://actioncivicscollaborative.org/wp-content/uploads/2013/07/EF_2013-curriculum-overview.pdf on February 6, 2021.

Facing History and Ourselves. (n.d.a). *Contracting.* Accessed at www.facinghistory.org/resource-library/teaching-strategies/contracting on October 15, 2021.

Facing History and Ourselves. (n.d.b). *Democracy and civic engagement.* Accessed at www.facinghistory.org/topics/democracy-civic-engagement on March 5, 2021.

Facing History and Ourselves. (n.d.c). *The power of images.* Accessed at www.facinghistory.org/resource-library/facing-ferguson-news-literacy-digital-age/power-images on March 5, 2021.

Facing History and Ourselves. (2016). *Fostering civil discourse: A guide for classroom conversations.* Accessed at www.facinghistory.org/sites/default/files/publications/Fostering_Civil_Discourse.pdf on March 5, 2021.

Facing History and Ourselves. (2021, January 11). *What happened during the insurrection at the US capital and why?* Accessed at www.facinghistory.org/educator-resources/current-events/what-happened-during-insurrection-us-capitol-why on March 5, 2021.

FactCheck.org. (n.d.). *Our mission.* Accessed at www.factcheck.org/about/our-mission on March 9, 2021.

Factitious. (n.d.). *Factitious 2020: Pandemic edition.* Accessed at http://factitious-pandemic.augamestudio.com/# on March 24, 2021.

Fallacy. (n.d.). In *Merriam-Webster's online dictionary.* Accessed at www.merriam-webster.com/dictionary/fallacy on October 15, 2021.

Farley, R. (2021, March 2). *Pace of U.S. vaccinations vs. the world.* Accessed at www.factcheck.org/2021/03/pace-of-u-s-vaccinations-vs-the-world on March 9, 2021.

Farnam Street Media. (n.d.). *How filter bubbles distort reality: Everything you need to know.* Accessed at https://fs.blog/filter-bubbles on December 20, 2021.

Federal Election Commission. (n.d.). *Official 2020 presidential general election results.* Accessed at www.fec.gov/resources/cms-content/documents/2020presgeresults.pdf on April 4, 2022.

Field, K. (2021, August 1). Teaching "action civics" engages kids—and ignites controversy. *The Hechinger Report.* Accessed at https://hechingerreport.org/teaching-action-civics-engages-kids-and-ignites-controversy on January 7, 2022.

Funk, C. (2020, February 12). *Key findings about Americans' confidence in science and their views on scientists' role in society.* Accessed at www.pewresearch.org/fact-tank/2020/02/12/key-findings-about-americans-confidence-in-science-and-their-views-on-scientists-role-in-society on April 19, 2021.

Games for Change. (n.d.a). *About us.* Accessed at www.gamesforchange.org/who-we-are/about-us on March 24, 2021.

Games for Change. (n.d.b). *Build a better world.* Accessed at http://gamesforchange.org/studentchallenge/build-a-better-world on March 25, 2021.

Games for Change. (n.d.c). *Fake it to make it*. Accessed at www.gamesforchange.org/game/game-4/#:~:text=Fake%20It%20To%20Make%20It%20is%20a%20simulation%2Dstyle%20game,they%20encounter%20in%20the%20future on March 24, 2021.

Games for Change. (n.d.d). *Games*. Accessed at www.gamesforchange.org/games on March 24, 2021.

Games for Change. (n.d.e). *National Games for Change student challenge*. Accessed at http://gamesforchange.org/studentchallenge on March 25, 2021.

Generation Citizen. (n.d.a). *Anyla Unique Lee*. Accessed at https://generationcitizen.org/story/anyla-unique-lee on February 7, 2021.

Generation Citizen. (n.d.b). *Civics day*. Accessed at https://generationcitizen.org/our-approach/civics-day on March 25, 2021.

Generation Citizen. (n.d.c). *Lexie Tesch*. Accessed at https://generationcitizen.org/story/lexie-tesch on February 7, 2021.

Generation Citizen. (n.d.d). *Our solution: Action civics*. Accessed at https://generationcitizen.org/about-us/the-solution-action-civics on February 6, 2021.

Generation Citizen. (n.d.e). *Safiya Alsamarrai*. Accessed at https://generationcitizen.org/story/safiya-alsamarrai on October 8, 2021.

Generation Citizen. (2018). *DeNora Getachew shares recommendations with the New York City Charter Revision Commission*. Accessed at https://medium.com/generation-citizen/denora-getachew-shares-recommendations-with-the-new-york-city-charter-revision-commission-e188b8959bdc on December 20, 2021.

GenerationGenius. (2018, October 6). *Extreme weather for kids | hurricanes, tornadoes, lightning | science lesson | grades 3–5* [Video file]. Accessed at www.youtube.com/watch?v=JOMVKSNFtb4 on April 19, 2021.

Gilchrist, J., & Parker, E. (2014). Racial/ethnic disparities in fatal unintentional drowning among persons aged ≤29 years—United States, 1999–2010. *Morbidity and Mortality Weekly Report, 63*(19), 421–426. Accessed at www.cdc.gov/mmwr/preview/mmwrhtml/mm6319a2.htm on January 5, 2022.

Gimkit. (n.d.). *Gimkit live*. Accessed at www.gimkit.com/product/live on March 24, 2021.

Gould, J., Jamieson, K. H., Levine, P., McConnell, T., & Smith, D. B. (Eds.). (2011). *Guardian of democracy: The civic mission of schools*. Accessed at https://media.carnegie.org/filer_public/ab/dd/abdda62e-6e84-47a4-a043-348d2f2085ae/ccny_grantee_2011_guardian.pdf on January 14, 2021.

Guilfoile, L., & Delander, B. (2014). *Six proven practices for effective civic learning*. Denver, CO: Education Commission of the States. Accessed at www.ecs.org/wp-content/uploads/Six-proven-practices-update_r2.pdf on January 17, 2022.

Haberman, C. (2015, February 1). *A discredited vaccine study's continuing impact on public health*. Accessed at www.retroreport.org/articles/a-discredited-vaccine-study-s-continuing-impact-on-public-health on October 15, 2021.

Hansen, M., Levesque, E., Valant, J., & Quintero, D. (2018). *The 2018 Brown Center report on American education: How well are American students learning?* Washington, DC: Brookings Institution. Accessed at www.brookings.edu/wp-content/uploads/2018/06/2018-Brown-Center-Report-on-American-Education_FINAL1.pdf on October 15, 2021.

Harper, F., Kamikawa, K., & Biaou, A. (n.d.). *Circles + community livability*. Accessed at https://francesharper.com/lesson-plans/geometry/circles-community-livability on April 19, 2021.

HHMI BioInteractive. (n.d.a). *BiomeViewer*. Accessed at www.biointeractive.org/classroom-resources/biomeviewer on April 22, 2021.

HHMI BioInteractive. (n.d.b). *The Anthropocene: Human impact on the environment.* Accessed at www.biointeractive.org/classroom-resources/anthropocene-human-impact-environment on October 8, 2021.

Holan, A. D. (2020, October 27). *The principles of the Truth-O-Meter: PolitiFact's methodology for independent fact-checking.* Accessed at www.politifact.com/article/2018/feb/12/principles-truth-o-meter-politifacts-methodology-i/#Our%20ownership on March 9, 2021.

Holcomb, S., Klebahn, P., Segovia, K., & Utley, J. (2017). *d.bootcamp 25.* Accessed at https://static1.squarespace.com/static/57c6b79629687fde090a0fdd/t/59bc54422aeba555ff0041fe/1505514587533/MASTER+DECK_2017+Sept+25+Bootcamp.pdf on January 28, 2022.

Holland, B. R. (2021, January 12). *We were warned.* Accessed at http://brholland.com/we-were-warned on October 15, 2021.

Hone, B. (2018, October 2). *How to play the Factitious 2018 news game.* Accessed at https://medium.com/@bobhone.designer/how-to-play-the-factitious-2018-news-game-9969aaa8f2a7 on March 24, 2021.

iCivics. (n.d.a). *Cast your vote.* Accessed at www.icivics.org/node/2190/resource?referer=curriculum/play/all&page_title=Curriculum%20All%20Games on March 21, 2021.

iCivics. (n.d.b). *Counties work.* Accessed at www.icivics.org/games/counties-work on April 22, 2021.

iCivics. (n.d.c). *Do I have a right?* Accessed at www.icivics.org/games/do-i-have-right on October 8, 2021.

iCivics. (n.d.d). *Executive command.* Accessed at www.icivics.org/games/executive-command on October 8, 2021.

iCivics. (n.d.e). *Games page.* Accessed at www.icivics.org/games on February 2, 2021.

iCivics. (n.d.f). *Step five: All about public policy.* Accessed at www.icivics.org/teachers/lesson-plans/step-five-all-about-public-policy?referer=node/273155&page_title=County%20Solutions%20Civic%20Action%20Plan on April 20, 2021.

iCivics. (n.d.g). *Who we are.* Accessed at www.icivics.org/who-we-are on March 20, 2021.

Ingraham, C. (2015, March 1). This is the best explanation of gerrymandering you will ever see: How to steal an election—A visual guide. *The Washington Post.* Accessed at www.washingtonpost.com/news/wonk/wp/2015/03/01/this-is-the-best-explanation-of-gerrymandering-you-will-ever-see on December 23, 2021.

International Energy Agency. (n.d.). *IEA atlas of energy.* Accessed at http://energyatlas.iea.org/#!/tellmap/1378539487/0 on April 30, 2021.

iThrive Games. (n.d.). *Lives in balance.* Accessed at https://ithrivegames.org/ithrive-sim/lives-in-balance on March 22, 2021.

Jamieson, K. H. (2013, Spring). The challenges facing civic education in the 21st century. *Daedalus, the Journal of the American Academy of Arts and Sciences, 142*(2), 65–83. Accessed at shorturl.at/bqwyO on January 11, 2022.

Johnston, M. (1957). *Roman life.* Chicago: Scott Foresman.

Jones, J. (2020, December 7). *In election 2020, how did the media, electoral process fare? Republicans, Democrats disagree.* Accessed at https://knightfoundation.org/articles/in-election-2020-how-did-the-media-electoral-process-fare-republicans-democrats-disagree on January 11, 2022.

Jurkowitz, M., & Mitchell A. (2020, February 5). *A sore subject: Almost half of Americans have stopped talking politics with someone.* Accessed at www.pewresearch.org/journalism/2020/02/05/a-sore-subject-almost-half-of-americans-have-stopped-talking-politics-with-someone on January 13, 2022.

Kachwaha, T. (2002). *Exploring the differences between discussion, debate, and dialogue.* Accessed at https://teaching.yale-nus.edu.sg/wp-content/uploads/sites/25/2016/04/Exploring-the-Differences-Between-Discussion-Debate-and-Dialogue.pdf on January 31, 2022.

Kahkajian, Y. (2021, March 3). *No, 5 UK nurses did not die from the COVID-19 vaccine.* Accessed at www.poynter.org/tfcn/2021/no-5-uk-nurses-did-not-die-from-the-covid-19-vaccine on March 6, 2021.

Kahoot! (n.d.). *How it works.* Accessed at https://kahoot.com/schools/how-it-works on March 24, 2021.

Kang, C., & Frenkel, S. (2020, July 14). 'PizzaGate' conspiracy theory thrives anew in the TikTok era. *The New York Times.* Accessed at www.nytimes.com/2020/06/27/technology/pizzagate-justin-bieber-qanon-tiktok.html on February 22, 2021.

Kang, C., & Goldman, A. (2016, December 5). In Washington pizzeria attack, fake news brought real guns. *The New York Times.* Accessed at www.nytimes.com/2016/12/05/business/media/comet-ping-pong-pizza-shooting-fake-news-consequences.html?searchResultPosition=12 on February 22, 2021.

Kavanagh, J., & Rich, M. D. (2018). *Truth decay: An initial exploration of the diminishing role of facts and analysis in American public life.* Santa Monica, CA: RAND Corporation. Accessed at www.rand.org/pubs/research_reports/RR2314.html on February 22, 2021.

Kemper, D., Meyer, V., Van Rys, J., & Sebranek, P. (2018). *Fusion: Integrated reading and writing, book 2.* Boston: Cengage Learning.

Khan Academy. (n.d.). *Protecting biodiversity: Local and global policies* [Video file]. Accessed at www.khanacademy.org/science/high-school-biology/hs-ecology/hs-human-impact-on-ecosystems/v/protecting-biodiversity-local-and-global-policies on April 20, 2021.

Kidizenship. (n.d.a). *About.* Accessed at www.kidizenship.com/about on March 25, 2021.

Kidizenship. (n.d.b). *All contests.* Accessed at www.kidizenship.com/all-contests on March 25, 2021.

Kissel, A. (2019, December 3). *Action civics for conservatives.* Accessed at https://townhall.com/columnists/adamkissel/2019/12/03/action-civics-for-conservatives-n2557413 on February 7, 2021.

Kleven, S. (2021, October 28). *Building a positive school climate through restorative practices.* Accessed at https://learningpolicyinstitute.org/product/wce-positive-school-climate-restorative-practices-brief on January 5, 2021.

Knight Foundation. (2018, October 4). *Disinformation, 'fake news' and influence campaigns on Twitter.* Accessed at https://knightfoundation.org/reports/disinformation-fake-news-and-influence-campaigns-on-twitter on February 22, 2021.

Konish, L. (2021, March 7). *Biden calls on Congress to restore Voting Rights Act, signs orders to help expand access.* Accessed at www.cnbc.com/2021/03/07/biden-calls-to-restore-voting-rights-act-signs-order-to-expand-access.html on October 7, 2021.

Kupchik, A., & Catlaw, T. J. (2015). Discipline and participation: The long-term effects of suspension and school security on the political and civic engagement of youth. *Youth and Society, 47*(1), 95–124.

Lai, P. F. (2018). *Civics English: Integrating civics in middle school English language arts teaching.* Doctoral dissertation, University of California, Berkeley. Accessed at https://escholarship.org/uc/item/50192908 on October 13, 2021.

The Learning Network. (2021, April 8). What's going on in this graph? Global life expectancy & health expenditures—How has the relationship between life expectancy and health expenditures by country changed since 2000? *The New York Times.* Accessed at www.nytimes.com/2021/04/08/learning/whats-going-on-in-this-graph-global-life-expectancy-heath-expenditures.html on April 22, 2021.

Leskes, A. (2013). A plea for civil discourse: Needed, the academy's leadership. *Liberal Education, 99*(4). Accessed at www.csmsg.org/wp-content/uploads/2016/12/AACU-article.pdf January 11, 2022.

Levine, L. (2020, December 2). *How to gather the oral histories of COVID-19.* Accessed at https://daily.jstor.org/how-to-gather-the-oral-histories-of-covid-19 on October 15, 2021.

Levine, P., & Kawashima-Ginsberg, K. (2015). *Civic education and deeper learning.* Boston: Jobs for the Future. Accessed at https://files.eric.ed.gov/fulltext/ED559676.pdf on February 5, 2021.

Levine, P., & Kawashima-Ginsberg, K. (2017). *The republic is (still) at risk—and civics is part of the solution*. Accessed at www.civxnow.org/sites/default/files/resources/SummitWhitePaper.pdf on January 15, 2021.

Lindsey, R., & Dahlman, L. (2021, March 15). *Climate change: Global temperature*. Accessed at shorturl.at/ryzFI on April 30, 2021.

Los Angeles Times. (2019, September 27). *Young activist makes strong speech to U.N. about climate change*. Accessed at https://newsela.com/read/Greta-UN-climate-summit/id/57716 on April 30, 2021.

Lumen Learning. (n.d.). *Identify common logical fallacies*. Accessed at https://courses.lumenlearning.com/olemiss-writ250/chapter/identify-logical-common-fallacies on October 15, 2021.

Madhani, A. (2021, March 7). *Biden marks 'Bloody Sunday' by signing voting rights order*. Accessed at https://apnews.com/article/joe-biden-alabama-selma-voting-rights-elections-eec9cde9f9713183b6c8d1d7123cbbae on October 7, 2021.

Mansky, J. (2018, May 7). The age-old problem of "fake news." *Smithsonian Magazine*. Accessed at www.smithsonianmag.com/history/age-old-problem-fake-news-180968945 on October 11, 2021.

Massachusetts Department of Elementary and Secondary Education. (2020). *The civics project guidebook*. Accessed at www.doe.mass.edu/frameworks/hss/civics-guidance.docx on December 20, 2021.

McLeod, S., & Shareski, D. (2018). *Different schools for a different world*. Bloomington, IN: Solution Tree Press.

Media Literacy Now. (2020). *U.S. media literacy policy report 2020*. Watertown, MA: Author. Accessed at https://medialiteracynow.org/wp-content/uploads/2020/01/U.S.-Media-Literacy-Policy-Report-2020.pdf on February 22, 2021.

Mehta, J., & Fine, S. (2019). *In search of deeper learning: The quest to remake the American high school*. Cambridge, MA: Harvard University Press.

Merriam-Webster. (n.d.). *The real story of 'fake news.'* Accessed at www.merriam-webster.com/words-at-play/the-real-story-of-fake-news on February 22, 2021.

Mikva Challenge. (n.d.a). *Our curricula*. Accessed at https://mikvachallenge.org/curricula on February 6, 2021.

Mikva Challenge. (n.d.b). *Project soapbox*. Accessed at https://mikvachallenge.org/our-work/programs/project-soapbox on March 25, 2021.

Mikva Challenge. (n.d.c). *Showcasing youth action*. Accessed at https://mikvachallenge.org/our-work/programs/action-civics-classrooms/showcasing-youth-action on February 7, 2021.

Mikva Challenge. (n.d.d). *Soapbox nation*. Accessed at https://mikvachallenge.org/soapbox-nation on March 25, 2021.

Miranda, L. (2016). *Hamilton*: An American musical. In J. McCarter (Ed.), *Hamilton: The revolution* (pp. 23–26). New York: Grand Central Publishing.

National Council for the Social Studies. (n.d.). *National curriculum standards for social studies: Chapter 2—The themes of social studies*. Accessed at www.socialstudies.org/national-curriculum-standards-social-studies-chapter-2-themes-social-studies on April 30, 2021.

National Council for the Social Studies. (2013). *The College, Career, and Civic Life (C3) Framework for Social Studies State Standards*. Accessed at www.socialstudies.org/standards/c3#:~:text=Download%20the%20C3%20Framework on January 14, 2022.

National Geographic. (2017, August 28). *Causes and effects of climate change* [Video file]. Accessed at www.youtube.com/watch?v=G4H1N_yXBiA on April 30, 2021.

National Governors Association Center for Best Practices & Council of Chief State School Officers. (2010a). *Common Core State Standards for English language arts and literacy in history/social studies, science, and technical subjects.* Washington, DC: Authors. Accessed at www.corestandards.org/assets/CCSSI_ELA%20Standards.pdf on October 7, 2021.

National Governors Association Center for Best Practices & Council of Chief State School Officers. (2010b). *Common Core State Standards for mathematics.* Washington, DC: Authors. Accessed at www.corestandards.org/assets/CCSSI_Math%20Standards.pdf on October 7, 2021.

NB Staff. (2021, March 3). *New MRC poll proves media's Cuomo cover-up distorted public's view.* Accessed at www.newsbusters.org/blogs/nb/nb-staff/2021/03/03/new-mrc-poll-proves-medias-cuomo-cover-distorted-publics-view on March 9, 2021.

New York City Department of Education. (n.d.). *January 6, 2021.* Accessed at https://infohub.nyced.org/in-our-schools/programs/january-6-2021 on March 10, 2021.

The New York Times. (n.d.). *National exit polls: How different groups voted.* Accessed at www.nytimes.com/interactive/2020/11/03/us/elections/exit-polls-president.html on April 21, 2021.

News Literacy Project. (n.d.a). *About.* Accessed at https://newslit.org/about on October 13, 2021.

News Literacy Project. (n.d.b). *Classroom activity: Is it "checkable"?* Accessed at https://newslit.org/educators/resources/classroom-activity-is-it-checkable on April 4, 2021.

News Literacy Project. (n.d.c). *Newslit nation.* Accessed at https://newslit.org/newslit-nation on February 22, 2021.

News Literacy Project. (n.d.d). *Resource library.* Accessed at https://newslit.org/educators/resources on February 22, 2021.

News Literacy Project. (n.d.e). *The sift archives.* Accessed at https://newslit.org/educators/sift on February 22, 2021.

NewseumED. (n.d.a). *About NewseumED.* Accessed at www.newseumed.org/about-newseumed on March 4, 2021.

NewseumED. (n.d.b). *Our EDCollections.* Accessed at www.newseumed.org/our-edcollections on March 8, 2021.

NewseumED. (n.d.c). *Propaganda through history: Analyzing historical sources.* Accessed at https://newseumed.org/tools/lesson-plan/propaganda-through-history-analyzing-historical-sources on March 6, 2021.

Next Generation Science Standards. (n.d.a). *3-5-ETS1 engineering design.* Accessed at www.nextgenscience.org/dci-arrangement/3-5-ets1-engineering-design on April 30, 2021.

Next Generation Science Standards. (n.d.b). *3-ESS3-1 earth and human activity.* Accessed at www.nextgenscience.org/pe/3-ess3-1-earth-and-human-activity on April 22, 2021.

Next Generation Science Standards. (n.d.c). *HS-LS2-8 ecosystems: Interactions, energy, and dynamics.* Accessed at www.nextgenscience.org/pe/hs-ls2-8-ecosystems-interactions-energy-and-dynamics on October 13, 2021.

Next Generation Science Standards. (n.d.d). *MS-ESS3-4 earth and human activity.* Accessed at www.nextgenscience.org/pe/ms-ess3-4-earth-and-human-activity on October 13, 2021.

No Child Left Behind (NCLB) Act of 2001, Pub. L. No. 107-110, § 115, Stat. 1425 (2002).

Northeast States Emergency Consortium. (n.d.). *Winter storms.* Accessed at http://nesec.org/winter-storms/#:~:text=Large%20winter%20storms%20can%20be,houses%20and%20making%20roads%20impassible on April 20, 2021.

Nunez, C. (2019, May 13). Carbon dioxide levels are at a record high. Here's what you need to know. *National Geographic.* Accessed at www.nationalgeographic.com/environment/article/greenhouse-gases on April 30, 2021.

Office of the Historian. (n.d.). *U.S. diplomacy and yellow journalism, 1895–1898*. Accessed at https://history.state.gov/milestones/1866-1898/yellow-journalism on February 22, 2021.

Oliver, J. (2015, April 2). *Red-tailed hawks: Last week tonight with John Oliver* [Video file]. Accessed at www.youtube.com/watch?v=uiN_-AEhTpk on February 21, 2021.

Ontario Ministry of Education. (2006). *The Ontario curriculum grades 1–8 language*. Accessed at www.edu.gov.on.ca/eng/curriculum/elementary/language18currb.pdf on January 14, 2022.

Ontario Ministry of Education. (2007). *The Ontario curriculum grades 11 and 12: English*. Accessed at www.edu.gov.on.ca/eng/curriculum/secondary/english1112currb.pdf on January 15, 2022.

Ontario Ministry of Education. (2013). *The Ontario curriculum grades 9 and 10: Canadian and world studies*. Accessed at www.edu.gov.on.ca/eng/curriculum/secondary/canworld910curr2013.pdf on January 4, 2022.

Ontario Ministry of Education. (2015). *The Ontario curriculum grades 11 and 12: Canadian and world studies*. Accessed at www.edu.gov.on.ca/eng/curriculum/secondary/2015cws11and12.pdf on January 14, 2022.

Ontario Ministry of Education. (2016). *The Ontario curriculum grades 9 to 12: Classical studies and international languages*. Accessed at www.edu.gov.on.ca/eng/curriculum/secondary/classiclang912curr.pdf on January 14, 2022.

Ontario Ministry of Education. (2018). *The Ontario curriculum: Social studies, grades 1 to 6; history and geography, grades 7 and 8*. Accessed at www.edu.gov.on.ca/eng/curriculum/elementary/social-studies-history-geography-2018.pdf on January 14, 2022.

Ontario Ministry of Education. (2021). *Social-emotional learning (SEL) skills*. Accessed at www.ontario.ca/document/health-and-physical-education-grades-1-8/social-emotional-learning-sel-skills on December 31, 2021.

PBS LearningMedia. (n.d.). *Human activities that threaten biodiversity* [Video file]. Accessed at https://mass.pbslearningmedia.org/resource/human-activities-that-threaten-biodiversity/biodiversity-videos on April 18, 2021.

People for Education. (2019, February 19). *What is civic literacy and why do our kids need it?* Accessed at https://peopleforeducation.ca/our-work/what-is-civic-literacy-and-why-do-our-kids-need-it on December 31, 2021.

Pew Research Center. (2018a, June 18). *Distinguishing between factual and opinion statements in the news*. Accessed at www.pewresearch.org/journalism/2018/06/18/distinguishing-between-factual-and-opinion-statements-in-the-news on December 20, 2021.

Pew Research Center. (2018b, June 18). *Quiz: How well can you tell factual from opinion statements?* Accessed at www.pewresearch.org/quiz/news-statements-quiz on March 4, 2021.

Pierce, O., Larson, J., & Beckett, L. (2011). *Redistricting, a devil's dictionary*. Accessed at www.propublica.org/article/redistricting-a-devils-dictionary January 11, 2022.

Poynter. (n.d.a). *MediaWise for Gen Z*. Accessed at www.poynter.org/mediawise-for-gen-z on March 6, 2021.

Poynter. (n.d.b). *MediaWise teen fact-checking network*. Accessed at www.poynter.org/teen-fact-checking-network on March 6, 2021.

Putnam, R. D. (1995). Bowling alone: America's declining social capital. *Journal of Democracy*, 6(1), 223–234.

Quizizz. (n.d.). *Teachers*. Accessed at https://quizizz.com/teachers on March 24, 2021.

Quizlet. (n.d.). *Quizlet live*. Accessed at https://quizlet.com/features/live on March 24, 2021.

Ramer, H. (2019, March 20). *Live free and fly: N.H. house approves state raptor.* Accessed at www.concordmonitor.com/Live-Free-and-Fly-New-Hampshire-House-approves-state-raptor-24275062 on January 17, 2020.

Raygoza, M. C. (2019). *Quantitative civic literacy.* Accessed at https://educate.bankstreet.edu/cgi/viewcontent.cgi?article=1275&context=occasional-paper-series on October 13, 2021.

Reagan, R. (1988, September 10). *Radio address to the nation on education.* Accessed at www.reaganlibrary.gov/archives/speech/radio-address-nation-education-3 on February 21, 2021.

Red & Blue Works. (2019). *From civic education to a civic learning ecosystem: A landscape analysis and case for collaboration.* Accessed at https://rbw.civic-learning.org/wp-content/uploads/2019/12/CE_online.pdf on January 14, 2021.

Retro Report. (n.d.). *Influencing public policy: Vaccines.* Accessed at www.retroreport.org/education/video/influencing-public-policy-vaccines on October 15, 2021.

Reuters. (2021, February 15). *Fact check: Courts have dismissed multiple lawsuits of alleged electoral fraud presented by Trump campaign.* Accessed at www.reuters.com/article/uk-factcheck-courts-election/fact-check-courts-have-dismissed-multiple-lawsuits-of-alleged-electoral-fraud-presented-by-trump-campaign-idUSKBN2AF1G1 on January 11, 2022.

Robert Wood Johnson Foundation. (n.d.). *Life expectancy: Could where you live influence how long you live?* Accessed at www.rwjf.org/en/library/interactives/whereyouliveaffectshowlongyoulive.html on April 19, 2020.

Rosenberg, S. (2019). *Democracy devouring itself: The rise of the incompetent citizen and the appeal of populism.* Accessed at www.researchgate.net/publication/331815844_Democracy_Devouring_Itself_The_Rise_of_the_Incompetent_Citizen_and_the_Appeal_of_Populism on January 17, 2022.

Rousseau, S., & Warren, S. (2018, March 20). *Civic participation begins in schools.* Accessed at https://ssir.org/articles/entry/civic_participation_begins_in_schools on October 13, 2021.

Rubin, B. C., & Hayes, B. F. (2010, September). "No backpacks" versus "drugs and murder": The promise and complexity of youth civic action research. *Harvard Educational Review, 80*(3), 352–379. Accessed at shorturl.at/cvwV9 on February 21, 2021.

Sadowski, A., & Martin, R. (2021, March 8). *COVID misinformation, racism, and propaganda: Fox News' newest show is already a disaster.* Accessed at www.mediamatters.org/brian-kilmeade/covid-misinformation-racism-and-propaganda-fox-news-newest-show-already-disaster on March 9, 2021.

Samara Centre for Democracy. (2019). *Investing in Canadians' civic literacy: An answer to fake news and disinformation.* Accessed at www.samaracanada.com/research/active-citizenship/investing-in-canadians'-civic-literacy on December 31, 2021.

Sawchuk, S. (2019a, July 17). How 3 states are digging in on civics education. *Education Week.* Accessed at www.edweek.org/teaching-learning/how-3-states-are-digging-in-on-civics-education on February 7, 2021.

Sawchuk, S. (2019b, November 26). Math: The most powerful civics lesson you've never had. *Education Week.* Accessed at www.edweek.org/teaching-learning/math-the-most-powerful-civics-lesson-youve-never-had/2019/11 on April 18, 2020.

Schudson, M. (1998). *The good citizen: A history of American civic life.* New York: Martin Kessler Books.

Service Learning Project. (2022). *Increasing voter education and turnout in NYC.* Accessed at http://servicelearningnyc.org/civic-engagement on January 5, 2022.

Shapiro, S., & Brown, C. (2018, February 21). *The state of civics education.* Accessed at www.americanprogress.org/article/state-civics-education on May 9, 2021.

Shenkman, R. (2019, September 8). *The shocking paper predicting the end of democracy.* Accessed at www.politico.com/magazine/story/2019/09/08/shawn-rosenberg-democracy-228045 on January 17, 2022.

Stanford History Education Group. (2016). *Evaluating information: The cornerstone of civic online reasoning*. Accessed at https://stacks.stanford.edu/file/druid:fv751yt5934/SHEG%20Evaluating%20Information%20Online.pdf on February 22, 2021.

Stanford History Education Group. (2020, January 16). *Sort fact from fiction online with lateral reading* [Video file]. Accessed at https://youtu.be/SHNprb2hgzU on April 30, 2021.

Stevens, H. (2020, August 7). A vaccine, or a spike in deaths: How America can build herd immunity to the coronavirus. *The Washington Post*. Accessed at www.washingtonpost.com/graphics/2020/health/coronavirus-herd-immunity-simulation-vaccine on October 15, 2021.

Strasburger, D. (2020, October 2). *So you want to work in political data*. Accessed at www.bluebonnetdata.org/post/so-you-want-to-work-in-political-data on April 22, 2021.

Taylor, M., Watts, J., & Bartlett, J. (2019, September 27). Climate crisis: 6 million people join latest wave of global protests. *The Guardian*. Accessed at www.theguardian.com/environment/2019/sep/27/climate-crisis-6-million-people-join-latest-wave-of-worldwide-protests on February 6, 2021.

Tremoglie, C. (2021, March 7). *Biden signs executive order to 'provide voting access' to citizens in federal custody*. Accessed at https://dailycaller.com/2021/03/07/biden-signs-voting-access-executive-order on October 7, 2021.

Tyack, D., & Cuban, L. (1995). *Tinkering toward utopia: A century of public school reform*. Cambridge, MA: Harvard University Press.

UNICEF Office of Global Insight and Policy. (2020). *Rapid analysis: Digital civic engagement by young people*. Accessed at www.unicef.org/media/72436/file/Digital-civic-engagement-by-young-people-2020_4.pdf on January 4, 2022.

Union of Concerned Scientists. (2022, January 14). *Each country's share of CO2 emissions*. Accessed at www.ucsusa.org/resources/each-countrys-share-co2-emissions on February 1, 2022.

United Nations. (2022). *The Paris Agreement*. Accessed at https://unfccc.int/process-and-meetings/the-paris-agreement/the-paris-agreement on February 2, 2022.

University of Wisconsin–Stout. (2020, June 1). *University archives collecting COVID-19 oral histories*. Accessed at www.uwstout.edu/about-us/news-center/university-archives-collecting-covid-19-oral-histories on March 30, 2022.

U.S. House of Representatives. (n.d.). *The Permanent Apportionment Act of 1929*. Accessed at https://history.house.gov/Historical-Highlights/1901-1950/The-Permanent-Apportionment-Act-of-1929 on January 14, 2022.

van der Voo, L. (2020, January 25). 'Kids are taking the streets': Climate activists plan avalanche of events as 2020 election looms. *The Guardian*. Accessed at www.theguardian.com/environment/2020/jan/25/climate-change-election-2020-youth-activism on February 7, 2021.

Vander Ark, T., & Leibtag, E. (2021). *Difference making at the heart of learning: Students, schools and communities alive with possibility*. Thousand Oaks, CA: Corwin Press.

Vasilogambros, M. (2021, October 18). *Bipartisan support for Red Flag laws wanes as GOP blocks bills*. Accessed at www.pewtrusts.org/en/research-and-analysis/blogs/stateline/2021/10/18/bipartisan-support-for-red-flag-laws-wanes-as-gop-blocks-bills on December 20, 2021.

Westheimer, J., & Kahne, J. (2004). What kind of citizen? The politics of educating for democracy. *American Educational Research Journal, 41*(2), 237–269.

Wexler, N. (2020, January 5). To educate good citizens, we need more than the 'new' civics. *Forbes*. Accessed at www.forbes.com/sites/nataliewexler/2020/01/05/to-educate-good-citizens-we-need-more-than-the-new-civics on February 7, 2021.

William and Flora Hewlett Foundation. (2013). *Deeper learning competencies*. Accessed at https://hewlett.org/wp-content/uploads/2016/08/Deeper_Learning_Defined__April_2013.pdf on February 6, 2020.

Wineburg, S. (n.d.). *What's at stake? Our democracy is at risk*. Accessed at https://cor.stanford.edu/whats-at-stake on February 22, 2021.

World Bank. (n.d.). *Population growth (annual %)*. Accessed at https://data.worldbank.org/indicator/SP.POP.GROW on April 20, 2021.

World Health Organization. (2020, September 23). *Managing the COVID-19 infodemic: Promoting healthy behaviours and mitigating the harm from misinformation and disinformation*. Accessed at www.who.int/news/item/23-09-2020-managing-the-covid-19-infodemic-promoting-healthy-behaviours-and-mitigating-the-harm-from-misinformation-and-disinformation on January 11, 2022.

Xu, J., Murphy, S. L., Kochanek, K. D., & Arias, E. (2020). *Mortality in the United States, 2018*. Accessed at www.cdc.gov/nchs/data/databriefs/db355-h.pdf on April 21, 2021.

Young-Saver, D. (2021, March 3). What does 95% effective mean? Teaching the math of vaccine efficacy. *The New York Times*. Accessed at www.nytimes.com/2020/12/13/learning/what-does-95-effective-mean-teaching-the-math-of-vaccine-efficacy.html on October 15, 201.

Zimmer, C. (2020, December 4). 2 companies say their vaccines are 95% effective. What does that mean? *The New York Times*. Accessed at www.nytimes.com/2020/11/20/health/covid-vaccine-95-effective.html on October 15, 2021.

INDEX

A
Abrams, Z., 63–64
action civics and authentic experiences
    about, 33–34
    action civics in action, 42–44
    action civics programs, 36–38
    best practices in civic education and, 28
    challenges of action civics, 45
    conclusion, 45
    considerations for the future of civics and, 138
    core components of quality action civics, 38–40
    deeper learning and, 35–36
    key takeaways for, 46
    technologies to enhance action civics, 40–41
    what works in civic education and, 24
    why of action civics, 34–35
activism, 34, 35
ad hominem, 52
analyzing historical sources, 70–71
appealing to ignorance, 52–53

B
best practices in civic education
    about, 23–24
    action civics and, 28
    courses on civics, government, law, related topics and, 25–26
    deliberations of current, controversial issues and, 26
    media literacy and, 27–28
    school climate reform and, 29
    service learning and, 26–27
    simulations of adult civic roles and, 27
    social-emotional learning (SEL) and, 28–29
    student voice in schools and, 27
bias, understanding bias, 68–69
Budin, H., 12–13

C
Center for Civic Education, 38
Checkology, 28, 69
citizenship, the making of good citizens, 11–13
civic action projects (CAPs), 44, 57–58
civic deserts, 10
civic education
    definition of, 1
    four dimensions of, 22
    how schools provide. *See* how schools provide civic education
    what works in. *See* what works in civic education
Civic Mission of Schools, The (Carnegie Corporation and CIRCLE), 3, 14–15, 23
civics lessons across subject areas. *See also* list of lessons
    English language arts. *See* English language arts
    interdisciplinary civics experiences. *See* interdisciplinary civics experiences
    science and mathematics. *See* science and mathematics
    social studies. *See* social studies
civil discourse
    about, 47–49
    addressing relevant, real-life problems, 51–52
    civic action projects (CAPs) and, 57–58
    conclusion, 60
    considerations for the future of civics and, 138
    controversial topics and, 58–60
    creating class norms and, 53–54
    debating different topics and, 52–53
    key takeaways for, 60–61
    participating in class dialogues and, 54
    participating in local government and, 50–51
    teaching democratic values through, 50–60
    virtual discourse and, 55–57
    why many teachers don't engage in, 49

clickbait, 70
close-reading strategies, 127–128
Cohen, C., 51
Collaborative for Academic, Social, and Emotional Learning (CASEL), 28
Constitutional Rights Foundation civic action projects, 44
Controlling the Spread of Misinformation (Abrams), 64, 66
COVID-19, 66
current events
    best practices in civic education and, 26
    traditional civics instruction and, 13–14

D

Dalmia, A., 80–81
debates
    and class norms, 53
    and deliberations of current, controversial issues, 26
    and dialogues, 54
    differences among discussion, debate, and dialogue, 55
    and the state of civic education, 2
    and teaching democratic values through civil discourse, 52–53
deeper learning and action civics, 35–36
democracy, definition of, 12–13
Democratic Knowledge Project, four dimensions of civic learning, 22
dialogue
    and civil discourse, 48
    and deliberations of current, controversial issues, 26
    differences among discussion, debate, and dialogue, 55
    and teaching democratic values through civil discourse, 54
discourse. *See* civil discourse
discussion
    and class norms, 53–54
    and controversial topics, 58–60
    differences among discussion, debate, and dialogue, 55
    and tools for collaboration, deliberation, and community outreach, 40
    and virtual discourse, 56–57
disinformation, 63

E

Earth Force, 38
elementary level civics lessons
    for English language arts, 98–103
    for interdisciplinary civics experiences, 123–129
    for mathematics, 115–118
    for science, 108–112
    for social studies, 88–91
engagement in civil discourse. *See* civil discourse
engagement through digital games and competitions. *See* games and competitions; list of games and competitions
English language arts. *See also* interdisciplinary civics experiences; list of lessons
    about, 97–98
    conclusion, 106
    elementary level civics lessons and, 98–103
    key takeaways for, 106
    secondary level civics lessons and, 103–106
epilogue
    call to action for parents, 141
    call to action for policymakers, 140–141
    call to action for school and district leaders, 140
    call to action for teachers, 139–140
    conclusion, 141
    considerations for the future of civics, 137–139
equity and civics education, 139

F

Factitious, 79
fake news, 64, 79
filter bubbles, 70

G

games and competitions. *See also* list of games and competitions
    about, 77
    competitions, 81–83
    conclusion, 83–84
    considerations for the future of civics and, 139
    digital games, 78–80
    key takeaways for, 84
Games for Change (G4C), 78–79, 83
Generation Citizen
    action civics and, 37, 42
    Generation Citizen Civics Day competition, 82
    story from the field, 43
Gould, J., 23
Guardian of Democracy (Gould), 23, 27

H

Hansen, M., 4
Holland, B., 18
how schools provide civic education
    about, 9–10
    civic education requirements, 15–19
    conclusion, 19
    key takeaways for, 19–20
    making of good citizens, 11–13
    modern civic engagement, 10
    traditional civics instruction, 13–15

I

iCivics, 27, 78
Informable, 79–80
Inglewood Gentrification, 44
institutional knowledge and civic literacy, 22
interdisciplinary civics experiences. *See also* list of lessons
    about, 123

conclusion, 135
elementary level civics lessons, 123–129
key takeaways for, 135
secondary level civics lessons, 129–135
introduction
about civic education, 1–3
about this book, 4–5
need for civic education reform, 3–4

J
justice-oriented citizen, 11–12

K
Kavanagh, J., 66
Kawashima-Ginsberg, K., 28–29, 34, 35, 36, 67
Kidizenship competitions, 83

L
lateral reading, 68
Let's Go There: Making a Case for Race, Ethnicity, and a Lived Civics Approach to Civic Education (Cohen), 51
Levine, P., 28–29, 34, 35, 36, 67
list of games and competitions
Agents of Influence, 81
Factitious, 79
Games for Change (G4C), 78–79, 83
Generation Citizen Civics Day competition, 82
iCivics, 27, 78
Informable, 79–80
Kidizenship competitions, 83
Lives in the Balance, 80
Project Soapbox, 37, 82–83
We the People: Mock Congressional Hearing competition, 81–83
list of lessons
climate science and our school, 124–129
community solutions to weather-related problems, 108–112
election demographics, 115–118
gerrymandering in the United States: curse or blessing? 91–95
leaders in our community, 88–91
mitigating human impacts on Earth's systems, 112–114
opinion writing and revising for the effective use of supporting facts, 98–103
policy, politics, and science of vaccines, 129–135
power of persuasion: advocating for change in the world, 103–106
zip code and life expectancy, 118–120
lived civics approach, 51
Lives in the Balance, 80
logical fallacies, 52–53

M
mathematics. *See* science and mathematics
McConnell, T., 15
McLeod, S., 36
media literacy. *See* news media literacy

Mikva Challenge, 37, 44
misinformation. *See also* news media literacy
about, 63–64
dangers of, 65–66
exposing motives of, 69–70
modern civic engagement, 10
modern civics in action
engagement in civil discourse. *See* civil discourse
engagement through digital games and competitions. *See* games and competitions
news media literacy for combating misinformation. *See* news media literacy
power of action civics and authentic experiences. *See* action civics and authentic experiences

N
news media literacy. *See also* misinformation
about, 63–65
action civics and, 35
best practices in civic education and, 27–28
civic literacy and, 22
conclusion, 74
considerations for the future of civics and, 139
dangers of misinformation and, 65–66
key takeaways for, 75
news media literacy activities, 67–72
news media literacy education, 66–67
tools to enhance online research and reasoning, 72–74
what works in civic education and, 24
news media literacy activities
analyzing historical sources, 70–71
exposing motives of misinformation, 69–70
lateral reading, 68
navigating digital information, 71
power of images, 71–72
understanding bias, 68–69
No Child Left Behind (NCLB) Act, 4, 14–15
norms, 53–54

O
Oliver, J., 51

P
participating in local government, 50–51. *See also* action civics and authentic experiences
participatory citizens, 11–12
personally responsible citizens, 11–12
Pew Research Center, 64, 72–73
Pizzagate conspiracy, 65–66
power of action civics and authentic experiences. *See* action civics and authentic experiences
Project Citizen, 38
Project Soapbox, 37, 82–83
project-based learning (PBL), 45
protests
action civics and, 35
January 6, 2021, 64–65

Q

quantitative civic literacy, 115

R

Raygoza, M., 114–115
Reagan, R., 49
red herrings, 53
Republic Is (Still) at Risk, The (Levine and Kawashima-Ginsberg), 28–29, 35, 67
resources
    for collaboration, deliberation, and community outreach, 40–41
    for communication tools for advocacy, 41
    for creating opportunities for dialogue, 56–57
    for elementary level civics lessons, 90–91, 103, 111–112, 118, 128–129
    for enhancing online research and reasoning, 72–73
    for fact-checking tools, 73–74
    for online research, 40
    for secondary level civics lessons, 94–95, 106, 114, 120–121, 134–135
Rich, M., 66
Rosen, J., 9
Rosenberg, S., 1

S

school climate reform, 25, 29
science and mathematics. *See also* interdisciplinary civics experiences; list of lessons
    about, 107
    civics in mathematics, 114–115
    civics in science, 108
    conclusion, 121
    elementary level civics lessons, 108–112, 115–118
    key takeaways for, 121
    secondary level civics lessons, 112–114, 118–120
secondary level civics lessons
    English language arts, 103–106
    interdisciplinary civics experiences, 129–135
    mathematics, 118–120
    science, 112–114
    social studies, 91–95
service learning, 14, 26–27
Shareski, D., 36
simulations of adult civic roles, 27. *See also* action civics and authentic experiences
social media. *See also* news media literacy for combating misinformation
    communication tools for advocacy and, 41
    misinformation and, 64
    modern civic engagement, 10
    news media literacy and, 24, 67
    virtual discourse and, 55, 57
social studies. *See also* interdisciplinary civics experiences; list of lessons
    about civics lessons for, 87–88
    conclusion, 95
    elementary level civics lessons, 88–91
    key takeaways for, 95
    secondary level civics lessons, 91–95
social-emotional learning (SEL), 25, 28–29
societal events and action civics, 35
Stanford History Education Group, 67
state of civic education
    how schools provide civic education. *See* how schools provide civic education
    what works in civic education. *See* civic education
straw man, 53
student voice in schools, 27

T

teacher tips
    close-reading strategies, 127–128
    digital station rotations, 114
    digital tools for data visualizations, 120
    digital tools for visible thinking and brainstorming, 110
    formative assessment practices, 117
    show, don't tell, 93
    student-centered learning experiences, 102
tools to enhance online research and reasoning, 72–73. *See also* resources
topical knowledge and civic literacy, 22
Trofi, M., 38
truth decay, 66

U

U.S. Citizenship and Immigration Services Naturalization Test, 15
U.S. presidential election 2020, 18, 64–65

V

virtual discourse, 55–57. *See also* civil discourse
voting rates, 2

W

We the People: Mock Congressional Hearing competition, 81–82
"We Were Warned" (Holland), 18
what works in civic education. *See also* civic education
    about, 21–22
    conclusion, 29
    implementation strategies for best practices in civic education, 25–29
    key takeaways for, 29
    promise and potential of schools, 22–25
Wineburg, S., 67

Equitable Instruction, Empowered Students
Carissa R. McCray
Learn practical strategies for ensuring each of your students feels valued, welcomed, and empowered. Author Carissa R. McCray provides the tools to combat biases inherent in education with pedagogy that encourages students to dismantle the injustices surrounding them.
BKG036

Growing Global Digital Citizens
Lee Watanabe Crockett and Andrew Churches
Discover how to transform education through the concept of global digital citizenship (GDC). Embraced by thousands of schools, GDC practices empower students to effectively and ethically participate in and contribute to the digital world around them.
BKF786

The Identity-Conscious Educator
Liza A. Talusan
Learn powerful, practical strategies for creating an inclusive school community and engaging in meaningful conversations to make this work successful. *The Identity-Conscious Educator* provides a framework for building awareness and understanding of five identity categories: race, social class, gender, sexual orientation, and disability.
BKG031

Finding Your Blind Spots
Hedreich Nichols
Author Hedreich Nichols infuses this book with a direct yet conversational style to help you identify biases that adversely affect your practice and learn how to move beyond those biases to ensure a more equitable, inclusive campus culture.
BKG022

Solution Tree | Press
a division of Solution Tree

Visit SolutionTree.com or call 800.733.6786 to order.

Wait! Your professional development journey doesn't have to end with the last pages of this book.

We realize improving student learning doesn't happen overnight. And your school or district shouldn't be left to puzzle out all the details of this process alone.

No matter where you are on the journey, we're committed to helping you get to the next stage.

Take advantage of everything from **custom workshops** to **keynote presentations** and **interactive web and video conferencing**. We can even help you develop an action plan tailored to fit your specific needs.

Let's get the conversation started.

Call 888.763.9045 today.

SolutionTree.com